THE RÔLE OF THE TEACHER IN THE INFANT AND NURSERY SCHOOL

The Rôle of the Teacher in the Infant and Nursery School

BY

DOROTHY E. M. GARDNER

AND

JOAN E. CASS

Department of Child Development
University of London Institute of Education

PERGAMON PRESS

OXFORD · LONDON · EDINBURGH · NEW YORK
TORONTO · SYDNEY · PARIS · BRAUNSCHWEIG

Pergamon Press Ltd., Headington Hill Hall, Oxford
4 & 5 Fitzroy Square, London W.1

Pergamon Press (Scotland) Ltd., 2 & 3 Teviot Place, Edinburgh 1

Pergamon Press Inc., 44-01 21st Street, Long Island City, New York 11101

Pergamon of Canada Ltd., 207 Queen's Quay West, Toronto. 1.

Pergamon Press (Aust.) Pty. Ltd., Rushcutters Bay, Sydney, N.S.W.

Pergamon Press S.A.R.L., 24 rue des Écoles, Paris 5e

Vieweg & Sohn GmbH, Burgplatz 1, Braunschweig

First edition 1965
Second impression 1968

Library of Congress Catalog Card No. 65-18638

PRINTED IN GREAT BRITAIN BY
C. TINLING & CO. LTD., LIVERPOOL, LONDON AND PRESCOT
08 002299 5

To the Nursery and Infant School teachers of this country with deep respect and in the hope that this book may be of help to them in their devoted work for young children.

Contents

Acknowledgements

THIS book makes mention of some of those who, in their writings and investigations, have illuminated our conceptions of the rôle of the teacher.

We wish, however, to record here our very warm thanks to the many head and assistant teachers who have so generously accepted our observers in their schools and given them information and every possible help.

We also wish to thank the many Local Education Authorities who have allowed us to observe in their schools.

Our grateful acknowledgements are also due to the many "Observers", all experienced teachers studying in the Department of childs Development. Their careful and patient hard work and enthusiasm has made this investigation possible, and their sympathy with the teachers they observed and admired enabled life in the Classrooms to go on naturally and without strain.

We are also very grateful to Dr. Ilse Hellman and to Dr. Doris Lee of the University of London Institute of Education, for helpful advice on this study, and to our colleague Mrs. Sylvia Gray for the contruction of the histograms.

CHAPTER I

Developments in English Infant and Nursery Schools and of the teachers' functions

DURING a professional life which began in 1921 I have witnessed great changes in education and particularly in Infant Schools.* It may well be that in the period ahead the very significant developments which are now so evident in Junior Schools may mean that the Infant Schools may cease to be the most rapidly changing part of the educational landscape. However, Infant Schools in considerable numbers began to reflect fundamental changes considerably earlier than did more than a few Junior Schools or Junior Departments of schools for children of a wider age range.

The Nursery School too has changed and developed, but as a younger institution it did not have so far to go. There never was a time when the Nursery School teacher's function was envisaged as chiefly that of a purveyor of information or moral training simultaneously to large numbers of relatively passive children. One has, however, only to open any textbook on the history of education to realise that for many years the Infant School teacher was expected to function in that way — in the nineteen-twenties it was still very common to find Infant teachers in front of their classes instructing and exhorting and, though often with great skill and warm humanity, trying to achieve the impossible task of securing uniformly good results from all members of the whole class. Oral lessons, usually short in duration, were interspersed with periods of physical activity or "occupation", but even in these periods the whole class would be engaged in the same series of physical exercises or the same "occupation". A considerable part of the teacher's time and energy was devoted to holding back the brighter children sufficiently to allow the more average ones to maintain the pace, while the rest of her exertions were particularly directed to the still more difficult problem of the backward children.

* In England, the Infant School provides for the education of children aged 5 to 7+ and the Junior School for children aged 7 to 11+. Nursery Schools cater for children under the age of 5.

1

Though faced with a host of formidable difficulties, one problem seldom troubled the minds of teachers, that of doubt or perplexity about their own function. The teacher in that period could have no doubts about her importance. She was very clearly indispensable. Moreover, the techniques of good class teaching were well established and mostly well known. In the nineteen-twenties, however, there were a few Infant Schools breaking away from the methods sometimes referred to as "Chalk and talk". The contribution of Montessori was probably the greatest single influence in this movement, though it was doubtless reinforced by the gradually increasing awareness of teachers of the work of psychologists engaged in constructing and applying "Intelligence Tests". These tests made it abundantly clear that the teacher, however able, could not or ought not to expect the same degree of achievement from all children of the same age. Sensitive teachers, however, had long been aware of so self-evident a fact — though the less sensitive had been inclined to blame the children and the over-sensitive to blame themselves.

Pioneer Infant teachers, such as Jessie Mackinder (whose book, *Individual Work in Infant Schools*, published in 1925 by the London Educational Publishing Co. was having a great influence in this country) were quick to appreciate what Montessori had illustrated. Namely, that it was possible even in large classes to have the children busily and purposefully occupied while the teacher could be in the background helping children individually, having previously devoted much time and thought to a careful preparation of the educational environment in the form of graded apparatus, much of which was largely self-teaching and self-corrective. Some schools adopted the Montessori material, but more often adapted it or supplemented it or evolved their own apparatus, occasionally relating some of it to the interests of their particular children as well as to their abilitites. The rôle of the teacher was therefore enlarged and expanded.

While it is probable that no good teacher of these methods could afford to be without the techniques of the good class teacher, additional skills were now required. Every fresh development in Infant School education seems to require additions to the equipment of a good teacher, but never the discarding of the qualities that made a really good teacher of the older methods. It does seem, however, that the emphasis may have altered to some extent and perhaps some teachers of quieter, less dramatic personality who would have been less valued in the days of class teaching, may be recognised as outstanding practitioners of modern methods — provided they have the art of organising and planning an environment suited to children and a deep understanding of the needs of the children as individuals.

A good teacher, however, will have vitality and enthusiasm, however quietly it is shown.

Of what seem to me to be the four major developments in Infant School education I have now touched on I and II, i.e. class teaching and individual work. Nursery Schools did not, I think, come into the picture till Stage II, though a reflection of the influence from Stage I was seen in the tendency to gather all the children together in groups for special activities more frequently than is done today. This tendency was, on the whole, more marked in teachers who had added a year of Nursery School training to an Infant School one or who had entered Nursery Schools without such a training, than in teachers whose whole training had been for Nursery School work. Stage III was brought about by the impact of the "project method" as emphasised by Dewey rather than Decroly, though some Infant School teachers showed interest in Decroly's methods and some influences from that source appeared in the schools. The soil was ready for some new seed, because a certain disillusion had arisen in relation to "Stage II" methods.

As always seems to happen, the early stages of a fresh approach are well carried out, because it is the pioneers who are responsible for them, i.e. the teachers who, from their own convictions have discarded some of the old methods and adopted, with careful thought, methods which they sincerely believe to be better for the children. These teachers have the courage to put up if necessary with opposition and criticism and will use these constructively, being ready to answer and to illustrate by good teaching that the fears of the critics are groundless. When, however, they have won their case and one-time opponents become inclined to support the changes, there is always a period when the new ideas are in danger, however good they may be. The danger comes from the practice of such methods by teachers who come to them from the desire to follow a fashion rather than from an inner conviction, therefore having only a partial understanding of the purposes and principles behind the methods.

For a time the less intelligent adherents to a method can do more harm than the opponents, and then some people are inclined to urge a return to the old ways. This, however, seldom happens, because it is, fortunately, not easy to submerge what is true. What gradually happens is that, while shorn of false and non-essential "trappings", the essence of each new influence inasmuch as it is based on the needs of children and on sound educational ideals, is assimilated into the educational ideas and practices of the school. We have never reverted to purely class teaching again in the Infant Schools though there was a time when critics of "Individual work" were loud in asserting that we should have to do so.

At that stage too often one found that less able teachers were concentrating so much on provision of apparatus that they forgot the needs of the children. Apparatus was available from publishing firms, often thoughtlessly provided and not critically watched. In those days, for example, it was quite a common experience to meet a child holding a picture and seeking for its label saying "Pl – Pl – " while trying to find the word "plate", whereas the publisher had assumed the word "dish" would be the one sought — and no teacher appeared to have anticipated such difficulties. A great deal of time was wasted, too, by labels being put into wrong envelopes or boxes, and conscientious teachers were faced with quite a serious problem in having to decide how much of their free time ought to be directed to the making, sorting and checking of apparatus rather than to other more important matters of preparation and enjoyment of a reasonable amount of leisure.

The problem was dramatically illustrated in the early days of the change-over from class teaching to individual work when Training Colleges appeared to turn into factories for the production of cards whenever a period of teaching practice was approaching or in progress. Exhausted students had no time to prepare stories, poetry or music or to think out their work for the coming day in a balanced way and approach the class with freshness and enthusiasm.

In due course teachers came to have access to good published material and learnt to use it selectively, making only such things themselves as were necessary to meet the purposes and interests of their own particular children.

It was in the strong emphasis which the "project" idea placed upon the purposes and interests of the learner that its great contribution lay. Progressive Infant teachers were quick to appreciate its value in that it harnessed to the cause of education the tremendous drive and energy of children when they are deeply concerned about finding out certain things and gaining certain skills for ends which they themselves appreciate.

The early interpretation of the project method, however, usually was that the teacher tried to find among the many interests of the children, one which not only appealed to all of them but would continue to do so over a considerable period — possibly a whole term — and was, moreover, rich in educational possibilities and provided opportunities for children of different abilities to make contributions at different levels. It is not difficult to realise that this phase, which I shall call "Stage III", required from the Infant teacher all the powers of leadership demanded by Stage I and also the organisation and study of the abilities of the children which were so necessary in Stage II.

Infant teachers, because of their independence from schools for older children, and also perhaps because of their tradition, were inclined to be the first to experiment with new ideas so although the earlier concepts of the project method would probably have been more suited to children of Junior School age, it was in the Infant Schools it was first most widely used. Once more the pioneers did most intelligent and successful work, while the later "followers" tended to stereotype schemes of work related to some "centre of interest" but omitted to consider the most vital question of its relation to the genuine purposes and interests of the children.

This tendency has caused the very word "project" to suffer rather undeserved condemnation from many teachers. It is not the word so much as the incorrect application of it that is at fault. The word, implying as it does purpose and planning to achieve specific ends, is probably more illuminating than the more vague label of "activities" which superseded it and which is no more clarifying than the earlier term "occupations".

The term "activities" has, however, perhaps one advantage, in that it suggests a variety of different purposes whereas the word "project" possibly suggests only one.

Good teachers in the Stage III (project) period were quick to realise that one main interest or purpose will not satisfy all the children, and particularly clearly was this the case with the five-year-olds. It was much to the credit of teachers that though they were often winning much approval and interest by their very skilful leadership, which produced at times most spectacular results, they themselves were aware that they were playing too dominant a rôle in order to keep all the children working with the same end in view, and that the real interests of certain children were either different from the beginning or became so after a much shorter period than the teacher was trying to maintain. Five-year-olds, even more than slightly older children, seem to need a variety of different experiences before they are ready to pursue more sustained interests and purposes. It is no doubt significant that neither Dewey nor Decroly considered the project method as applying to the education of children under six.

For the same reason Stage III never had a very fundamental influence on Nursery Schools. There were some Nursery School teachers who tried to introduce "projects" especially with four-year-old children, and I can even remember one Nursery School which based each week's programme on a "Centre of Interest". But these attempts to channel the interest of such young children into specific directions were clearly not successful, and teachers were quickly aware of the fact that what the children really wanted to do was generally equally rich in educational possibility if fostered and encouraged intelligently. Moreover, it was apparent that such things carried the great advantage of having the child's full co-operation and attention. On the whole Nursery Schools may, I think, be said to have begun at Stage II and passed on to Stage IV.

Stage IV evolved partly from Stage III. The recognition by Infant and Nursery School teachers of the variety of ways in which was made evident the enthusiasm of young children for finding out about the world around them and overcoming difficulties gave them an even deeper respect for the purposes of children and for their eagerness to learn, so that they began to allow the older as well as the younger Infant School children a greater variety of choice. Susan Isaacs's researches at the Malting House School in Cambridge, published in the nineteen-thirties, were becoming known to teachers and illustrated very clearly how often the highest peaks of the child's thought and learning were found in the situation of spontaneous and purposeful play. Teachers realised afresh what Froebel meant when he wrote of play that it is not "trivial" but "highly serious and of deep significance".

Nursery Schools had always provided periods for free play, although a sample programme of the Nursery School day, published in 1936, was found to devote only one half-hour to it each day, and when visiting Nursery Schools at that time one often found that one was not expected to want to watch free play periods. It would be suggested that one should arrive in time to see the children at work with graded apparatus, during music, story and language periods, at dinner and preparing for afternoon sleep. Free play usually took place before visitors came and after they left and was evidently not considered of paramount importance by the teachers. That position has drastically changed.

Apparatus designed to teach specific facts and to encourage specific types of perception or skill is still often available, but has now become a part only of a much richer and more varied environment. In Nursery Schools at least, free play has moved from the fringe into the heart of the curriculum. In Infant Schools too (though such terms as "Free activities", "Creative activities", "Free choice time", etc., may take the place of the word "play") it is increasingly common to find at least one hour a day devoted to a period in which children can choose their occupations and pursue them either individually or in larger or smaller groups as their purposes dictate.

Some Infant Schools have gone much farther than this and, like most Nursery Schools, devote most of the day to the children's free choice only making breaks when particular experiences which must be offered by the teacher are given, such as stories, poetry and listening to music. Reading, writing and arithmetic, creative music making, and practice of physical skills with apparatus are available at many times of the day together with the creative materials and dramatic properties which previously were more commonly associated with the idea of a free choice period.

Good teachers have done so much to foster the interests of the children and open up fresh possibilities to them that in some schools there is no need to safeguard particular "subjects" such as reading, writing and arithmetic by reserving special times for them, since the children can be relied upon to choose them sufficiently and sometimes for longer periods than would have been allocated by a time-table.

Many Infant Schools, however, still rely on a definite period for free choice and less able teachers sometimes leave this period in isolation from the rest of the time-table which loses some of its potential value as providing a motive and purpose for other work. Good teachers, however, are generally on the alert to notice both when things done by children in the free choice time are worthy of further opportunities for expansion during the day, and when they need enrichment from ideas provided at other times, such as by stories, talks, visits, etc.

As always, the less understanding teachers have caused Stage IV to incur considerable criticism, but again there are signs that good teachers will not be intimidated by statements that these methods have been tried and failed and "we shall have to go back to – ?" They have heard such remarks before and know that one does not go back but forward, incorporating always in every advance the features which were good and admirable from earlier stages.

The rôle of the teacher is, however, a still more composite one now and less easily understood. For that reason it seemed that a study of good teachers who achieve success might have much to offer at the present stage. There is still considerable misunderstanding about the teacher's function in the modern Infant School and even in the Nursery School, though, in the latter, the young child's obvious need for physical care and good mothering relieves the teacher to some extent both from outside criticism and from any doubts she may herself feel. The Infant School teacher, except perhaps in the reception class, has less of such protection. Parents, for example, may accuse her of doing nothing but just letting the children play, and extremists for ideas of freedom may make her very diffident about whether she ought to intervene.

It is so evident to the observer who is privileged enough to have long periods of watching a skilled Infant teacher at work that she is constantly participating in a sensitive and flexible way and always in partnership with the children. To such an observer it is clearly evident that the idea that the teacher is passive and the children evolve everything for themselves, or that the teacher must always domin-ate and direct, is far from the truth. Few people, however, have the opportunity of being present on many occasions until accepted by teacher and children as someone who is happy to be able to watch quietly, requiring no special attention, clearly not there to make criticisms but accepting the situation as it is, so that the teacher feels free to behave in her normal way.

Young students may at their first stage of training have such opportunities, but they are often too eager to be teaching and too inexperienced to observe as fully what the experienced teacher sees. Owing to a perfectly healthy tendency to idealism, they are often more inclined to feel critical of what falls short of perfection; this is a fact of which sensitive teachers are fully aware and generally able to tolerate with good humour. Nevertheless, it stimulates their sense of responsibility towards the observer, since the teacher knows that the young student needs to learn the techniques of teaching and may require explanations which would not be needed by experienced observers.

I felt that my own access to experienced teachers, taking the advanced course in Child Development in my department at the University of London Institute of Education, gave me an oppor-tunity of having the co-operation of teachers who were not only keen people wishing to continue their studies, but were also practising the techniques of careful observation, recording and making a study of methods of research. Moreover, I felt sure that the enquiry was likely to attract their co-operation. Though most of them have been recognised as gifted teachers for considerably more than the five years of experience which is the minimal requirement before taking this course, some of them had not had the experience of teaching in "progressive" Infant Schools. Others, who had had such experience were very eager for the opportunity to study the work of other teachers which is so seldom available to teachers once the first training period is finished. My expectations were justified in that over the years from 1950 to the academic year of 1961–62, the topic has seldom failed to find at least one and often several recruits.

My colleague, Miss Joan Cass, has also recruited many students who worked with her on a similar study of teachers in the Nursery School and has generously given me permission to include her records with mine. I have, however, reported her comments and often her findings separately from my own in order that her own work shall be clearly evident. Her approach was originally slightly different from my own, in that it was specially directed to the teacher's contri-bution to the social climate of the group of which she was in charge, whereas mine was more broadly towards the general function of the Infant School teacher. Miss Cass's study, however, involves so broad a concept of what makes a happy "social climate" and mine inevitably included the teacher's contribution to the social climate, so that to separate studies producing such similar evidence would be unnecessary and wasteful of the supporting evidence which each gives to the other.

In the earlier years of both studies, Miss Cass and I also enjoyed the very valuable co-operation of Dr. Ilse Hellman who was at that time a colleague in the Department of Child Development.

The methods we evolved will be described in a following chapter. Progress has perhaps been slower than was at first envisaged, not only because we found the need to abandon some of the earlier work as experience improved our techniques (especially in the analysis of records), but because our findings opened up further avenues which we wished to explore. Even now we should like to go on adding to these records and are aware that much still remains to be done. However, since the work so far accomplished gives a picture of the rôle of a considerable number of gifted Infant and Nursery School teachers and reveals not only the variations between the teachers but considerable features which they display in common, it seems a pity to withhold publication longer. I have been assured by many teachers that these findings will be of help to other teachers who, while sympathetic to recent advances in Infant School procedure, are as yet uncertain as to how far they should go in exercising leadership and control and who wish to know how this may be done without removing initiative and freedom to experiment from the children.

Moreover, this study owes so much to the kindness of so many good teachers that I feel a wish to acknowledge the hard work and patient self-criticism of the investigators and the willingness of the teachers to accept observers for long periods, and to answer their questions.

The best acknowledgement I can offer is to make available to others a study to which they have all contributed and which should reveal, it is hoped, at least a partially completed picture of the work of devoted teachers in Nursery and Infant Schools today. Such records, seen in relation to the work of other investigations, should speak more clearly than verbal argument to answer those who underestimate the contribution of the teacher, but it is to those who respect but seek to understand more fully that this study is particularly offered.

Miss Cass's comments are given below.

B

The Nursery School teacher's contribution

The idea of this particular study was to see if it would be feasible to discover and measure those qualities of personality which the good Nursery School teacher seems to possess in such abundance and which obviously affects so significantly the well being and happiness of the children in her care.

What does constitute the teacher's contribution to the social climate of the group of children of whom she is in charge? One has often seen groups of young children similar in age range, in physical environment and material equipment, and yet very different in social climate.

Obviously the difference must lie in the personality of the teacher herself, for a child's emotional tone, his feelings about himself, his self-confidence, self-respect, and his sense of security are deeply affected by the adult's attitude and behaviour towards him, and this in turn, will of course affect his behaviour towards others.

The example a teacher sets is often far more important than she herself realises, for young children particularly tend to take on the values and behaviour of those they are with. Children are, of course individuals, the majority of whom are nurtured within the setting of their own families, and the quality of the relationships which they form with adults and other children outside the home, and their mental health as a whole will depend to a very large extent on that which they experience within the family.

Some children will obviously find it more difficult than others to make happy and secure relationships and to develop into stable human beings because of both environmental and inherited factors. Although the home is the place which influences the child most, everyone with whom he comes in contact will make some kind of a contribution to his development, a positive or a negative one. Therefore the personality of the teacher with whom children often spend a considerable part of their day, particularly perhaps at the Nursery School and Infant School stage, when they are so dependent on the adult for support and understanding, will be of extreme importance.

A teacher's work and influence does not consist merely in providing factual material for children to absorb. True education embraces all aspects of development — emotional, social and physical, as well as intellectual.

A teacher's influence too so often extends from the child to his family for she is aware of how inseparable the two are. So, knowledge is shared, confidences are built up and warm and friendly contacts are established and maintained, so that home and school work together for the child's ultimate well being. This demands wisdom and maturity from the teacher. Lois Barclay Murphey, in her monograph "Social Behaviour and Child Personality", emphasises this point when she says, "Anyone who has observed a number of groups of children is aware of the way in which a blythe and affectionate adult may unconsciously release warm friendliness in a group of children, and how even unconscious adult tensions may create insecurity and, along with it, antagonistic and competitive behaviour in children."

It was to try to define and measure these qualities in the individual teacher to which children respond with obvious feelings of well being and satisfaction, and to measure also, where possible, those subtle qualities of temperament; such things as a teacher's vitality, spontaneity, buoyancy and gaiety, which exert their unconscious influence on children, that this particular study was devised.

To list the actual qualities desirable in a teacher is not, perhaps, such an impossible task. Arthur Jersild in his book, *When Teachers Face Themselves*, stresses the importance of self-awareness. "An essential function of good education", he says, "is to help the growing child to know himself and to grow in healthy attitudes of self acceptance. A teacher cannot make much headway in understanding others or in helping others to understand themselves unless he is endeavouring to understand himself. If he is not engaged in this endeavour he will continue to see those whom he teaches through the bias and distortions of his own unrecognised needs, fears, desires, anxieties, hostile impulses, and so on. The process of gaining knowledge of self and the struggle for self fulfilment and satisfaction is not something an instructor teaches others. It is something in which he himself must be involved."

Susan Isaacs, in *The Psychological Aspects of Child Development*, points out that it is "highly desirable that the educators of young children should have sufficient understanding of the psychological processes underlying the difficulties of behaviour to be able to exercise patience and understanding", so that they realise "that time and normal growth under favourable conditions will do much to relieve these difficulties". *The Nursery and Infant School Report** stipulates that: "The first essential for a teacher of young children is that she should have the right temperament. A teacher of young children should not only have a real love and respect for children, but should be a person of imaginative understanding, sympathy and balance."

One can find numerous other writers who describe what the good teacher should be and know. The problem, however, which we set

* Report of Consultative Committee, Ministry of Education, 1933.

ourselves here was in actually observing a living, human being, a teacher with a group of real flesh and blood children and in seeing and measuring those personal qualities and techniques which are felt to be really desirable and in interpreting them in relation to the children concerned.

CHAPTER II

Acknowledgement of some other work in this field

It is impossible in the space of this book to enumerate all the wise and discerning opinions expressed by educationalists, based on their sensitive observation of children and teachers influenced by their own values and concepts of education. Few writers either on the philosophy of education or on the techniques of progressive teaching have failed to appreciate the importance of the rôle of the teacher. To list even briefly such opinions, valuable as they are, would fill a volume and make wearisome reading by removing the views expressed from their context and setting. Many books quoted in the bibliography are listed because they are particularly illuminating on the teacher's rôle, although they do not deal with research in the narrower sense of that word.

A few examples may however be cited here as illustration:

1. That the importance of the teacher is recognised.

E. Mellor, *Education and Experience in the Infant School*, writes: "What then are the conditions which will be most conducive to security and stability in these young children? The first and most important factor is the teacher herself. The general atmosphere of the life of the classroom, which is an extension of the personality of the teacher, is next in importance for the child. The teacher has the most fundamental, far-reaching and direct influence on the children."

E. Warr, *Social Experiences in the Junior School*: "It must not be concluded that because stress is laid today on the importance of a suitable environment, that it is the materials which educate. The teacher herself is still the most important factor in the environment. Her personality, her quality of mind, her respect for the individuality of her children and the understanding of their needs that she brings to her work, whether she is teaching, directing, guiding or just giving help when required, have a profound influence."

2. That the varied nature of the teacher's function is taken into account.

Quoted by B. P. Stevens, *The Activities Curriculum in the Primary*

Grades: "A teacher is leader, chairman, chief interlocutor, coach, umpire, taskmaster, guide or friend as occasion may require."

3. That good teachers are prepared to wait for and co-operate with the children's experiments and ideas.

Hockett and Jacobson, *Modern Practices in the Elementary School*: "She (i.e. the good progressive teacher) recognises that tinkering and experimenting sometimes are valuable preliminary steps towards more definite purposes and achievements. . . . A teacher's passion for military, clockwork precision would deprive the children of the joys of discovering things for themselves. A wise teacher does not consider time wasted if she sees that the children are laying a foundation for more effective work later."

4. That the teacher's rôle is an active and purposeful one.

Woffard, *Teaching in Small Schools*: "On the whole, the most successful teachers are those who make the most careful plans for teaching. . . . The artist teacher frequently changes his plans to fit the interests and needs of his children. That he shifts his plan is important, but that he has a plan to shift is more fundamental."

5. That good teaching consists of a carefully thought out balance between respecting the purposes of children and giving necessary help, guidance and control.

This principle is laid down so frequently and so vividly by all serious studies of the principles and practice of progressive education that it is surprising to find that so much misunderstanding still exists. Two examples must suffice here:

N. P. Porter, *The Teacher in the New School*: "Her's (the teacher) is the responsibility for finding the conditions which stimulate self-educative activity and for co-operating in such a way that increased learning will result — lack of guidance by the teacher is just as unfortunate . . . as is extreme adult domination."

A. G. Melvin, *The Activity Program*: "It is in the initiation of activities, if anywhere that the teacher should keep hands off. Here more than anywhere else the teacher should wait for the children's responses. But is a teacher a passive agent even here? Far from it. She has already been active in preparing an environment which abounds with various stimuli to activity. She is active in awakening needs. Furthermore she arranges situations for discussion during which needs may be brought forward, recognised and evaluated and in the progress of which they may issue into purposes."

6. That progressive teachers are aware of the need at times to exert direct influence and control.

Dicke, *The Enterprise in Theory and Practice*: "The facts to be emphasised are that the child is always seeking after something and it is the teacher's art to direct the search so that the ensuing educational results may be those that society will commend."

And again:

"Although the teacher cannot choose the pupil's purpose, he can and continually does introduce new purposes into his field of choice and he can and does, by his personality and method of presentation, influence that choice."

A. G. Melvin, *The Activity Program*: "The teacher should reveal to the children under her charge good standards of judgement. It is but a poor service to the child to let him go wrong in what pretends to be his own interests."

To turn to the question of specific research on the rôle of the teacher there is less work to report, since the subject has not attracted a great wealth of the "laboratory" type of study. Even here, however, some selection has been made in order to emphasise work which is of special relevance to the teacher of children under eight working in schools of an "active" kind. Facilities for such studies have not been easily available for much more than thirty years, since, before then, schools of an "active" kind were not so plentiful.

The Nursery School, however, has offered such facilities for a longer time, and mention should be made of a study conducted in 1929–30 by Josephine Foster of the University of Minnesota. She investigated the distribution of the teacher's time among children in Nursery Schools and Kindergartens. This work involved recording the actions of the teachers, as well as noting to which children the attention was given in order to find out whether older or younger children, boys or girls, difficult or gifted children absorbed more time. Records were also taken of the purposes and situations of the teacher's intervention. This brings the work close to that of Miss Cass's Nursery School Study and of my own with five-year-old children. Since, however, the main purpose of the study was slightly different from ours, certain types of participation are recorded in less detail and others were recorded at different times in the daily programme from those which we decided to record.*

A. T. Jersild, B. Goldman, C. L. Jersild and J. C. Loftus† under-

* Josephine C. Foster, "Distribution of the teacher's time among children in the nursery school and kindergarten", *Journal of Educatonal Research*, 1930.

† Reported in the *Journal of Experimental Education*, Vol. IX, June 1941; Vol. X, Dec. 1941.

took two pieces of research in America at the beginning of the Second World War which have relevance to the rôle of the teacher in the active school, but this work was not done with children below the third grade (i.e. the eight-year-olds).

Twelve schools of a formal and twelve of an informal type were used in their first study, and four pairs of schools in the second study, the work involving sustained observation of the responses of teachers and children in sixteen classes (four in each school). The techniques employed in this second study were very similar to those I had decided to use and afforded encouragement to me when I subsequently read this report. I used a similar method of recording and then analysing the teacher's contributions into types of contribution by the teacher and interchanges between the teacher and children, but I found it desirable to employ a considerably larger number of categories of teachers' contributions in order to avoid distortion of the very varied and flexible range of contacts made by informal Infant School teachers. (I found it necessary to use nearly eighty categories whereas in the study by Jersild and his collaborators, forty-nine were found to be sufficient.)

It is possible that broader categories are more appropriate for describing the teacher's contributions in working with older children, but my aim was to illustrate in as much detail as possible the skills used by teachers using very informal methods with younger children. For the same reason I did not undertake my investigation in formal schools but used more than thirty schools of an informal type.

In the pilot stage of my study I attempted to use only forty categories, but found that agreement between assessors of each contact was very much higher when the eighty categories involving more specific description were employed. With this list of categories we were able to get an agreement of not less than 80 per cent as between five assessors. The more detailed description of each category seemed to remove ambiguities of interpretation. A difference in my results from those of the above study is that I found what might be described as "positive" attentions from the teachers considerably outweighed the "negative", though I did not specifically classify my results with the idea of comparing the positive with the negative contributions.

Another research which comes close to my own is that of H. H. Anderson and H. N. Brewer, who were later assisted by M. F. Reed.* Much of this work was undertaken with teachers of children under the age of eight and the method of taking samples of consecutive

* *Studies of Teachers' Classroom Personalities*, California Standard University Press, Applied Psychology Monographs I, II, and III; VI, VIII and XI, 1945–46.

records and later analysing them was in very close line with my own methods. The object of the study was somewhat different — to find what effect the classroom personalities of the teachers had upon the children, as well as (in common with my own object) to note similarities and differences in the type of teacher participation, which was necessary also for my main purpose of finding what are the characteristic practices of teachers already known to be successful in informal schools.

Again, a much smaller number of categories of different types of teacher contact was used than in my study and they were partially classified as "Dominative" and "Integrative", which I did not attempt to do. Work was done also with the children. The same teachers were followed up in subsequent years and the same children when in charge of other teachers.

Anderson and Brewer found that as much as 300 to 400 minutes of observation was necessary to obtain a high degree of consistency. This conclusion led me to experiment on my own method of recording nine 20-minute samples during periods of freely chosen activities by asking the five observers during one year to pay 15 instead of 9 visits to one of the three teachers when they were observing, thus achieving the minimum 300 minutes recommended by Anderson and Brewer. I then examined the proportional contacts of these five teachers as between the first period of 180 minutes and the whole 300 minutes of their records and found that the contacts revealed by my previous method of taking nine 20-minute samples of periods — spread equally between the beginning, middle, and ending, of the "free choice" time — differed very little in proportion to those taken in the fifteen periods. It therefore seemed wise to continue taking the nine samples, which enabled me to have access to a larger number of teachers than I could have done with the fifteen samples. Possibly my narrower task of sampling contacts made by the teacher only during the "free choice" period rather than throughout the day was the reason why the variation in the types of contact made by each teacher was more constant.

Another study which has much in common with mine is that of A. C. Jensen.* A sample of teachers was observed, and incidents of behaviour which appeared to differentiate effective from ineffective teachers were noted — about 500 incidents were collected and analysed and the results placed in three categories: (a) personal qualities, (b) professional qualities, (c) social qualities. Many of the qualities listed as of importance as requirements for good teaching would, if I had described them in more general terms, have been evident in my own study.

* *Journal of Experimental Education*, Vol. XX, 1951.

The list given by Jensen is:

1. Alert, cheerful and enthusiastic in expression and manner.
2. Exhibits self-control and good organisation ability in the midst of classroom demands.
3. Likes fun and possesses a sense of humour.
4. Recognises and admits own mistakes graciously.
5. Fair and impartial.

The professional qualities were:

1. Evidences a planned but flexible procedure anticipating individual needs and interests.
2. Stimulates pupils through interesting and original material and teaching techniques.
3. Conducts well-planned, clear, practical demonstrations and explanations.
4. Clear and thorough in giving directions.
5. Skilful in encouraging pupils to work through their problems and evaluate own work.
6. Disciplines in a quiet, dignified, positive and fair manner.
7. Gives constructive help willingly and enthusiastically.
8. Foresees and resolves potential difficulties.

Category (c) included:

1. Shows understanding and sympathy in working with pupils.
2. Friendly, democratic and courteous in relations with pupils.
3. Helps individuals with personal as well as educational problems.
4. Commends effort and gives generous praise for work well done.
5. Is able to anticipate reactions of others in social situations.
6. Encourages others to do their best.

A year before Jenson's work was published, P. M. Symonds* made observations on twenty-four teachers who were working in a variety of different types of school, including twelve who were teaching in elementary grades. He concluded that there was no "best" type of teacher but that even the smallest detail of a teacher's response in the class was a function of her personality.

While I should not dispute the above conclusion I believed that there might be more in common in the kind of techniques adopted by successful Infant School teachers using methods based on providing for, following up and stimulating, the interests and purposes of young children, and in this belief I was encouraged by a statement

* *Journal of Educational Research*, Vol. XLIII, p. 688, 1950.

made by R. P. Porter (*The Teacher in the New School*, World Book Co., 1931), "The teacher is principally responsible for the pupils' acquisition of knowledge and skill, for their formulation of the generalisations that will help them meet the problems of life, for giving practice in forming desirable habits and attitudes. Success in attaining these ends appears to be partly dependent . . . upon the development of a technique. Much of this technique seems to be peculiar, not to the teacher, but to the method. If that is true, an analysis of the way in which one teacher works with her pupils should be of help to other teachers."

My own hope was that by the analysis of the way in which thirty good Infant School teachers worked with their pupils, it might be possible to find a strong indication at least of the types of technique most important to success in informal teaching of young children, together with some illustration of the variety of ways in which different teachers, according to differences in personality, might emphasise certain techniques more than others.

Since my own work began I was further encouraged in this hope by the very interesting research of Marie Hughes of the University of Utah. She had a similar purpose to my own in that her work, which arose from a study of teaching conducted under the direction of the Utah State Merit Study Committee, was based on the belief that the research might lead to a definition of teaching more adequate than those available in the literature on the topic. The method used was similar to my own and consisted of recording teaching periods of thirty-five teachers, most of whom were selected as "good" teachers. The teachers were observed in three teaching situations, one of which was an activity period.

As in my work, too, the code for the analysis of teaching was evolved from the actual records and subsequently grouped, but under general categories rather different from the ones I used. Moreover, the children were a little older, aged from 7–10 years inclusive, whereas mine were under the age of eight, so there is only one year (7–8) where the ages are similar in the two studies. Some differences in the findings will no doubt be due to this and since the results are reported somewhat differently an exact comparison would require revision and regrouping of the whole of my records to bring them into line with those of Marie Hughes which would not be desirable after a lapse of time. The two studies have, however, much in common and I find her recommendations supporting to my study.*

* Marie R. Hughes, *Development of the Means for Assessing the Quality of Teaching in Elementary Schools*, U.S. Department of Health, Education and Welfare Office of Education, Washington 25, D.C., 1958–59.

In investigating the function of the teacher other methods have, of course, been used — I have expanded rather more on the above studies because they are mainly based on the recording and analysis of the teachers' behaviour in the classroom situation.

Other studies also such as those of Bernice Baxter, published in 1941*, have revealed the effects upon the children of the personality and behaviour of different teachers. This is, of course, a most important and interesting question, but not one which I attempted to answer in my own study.

Lewin, Lippett and White† also investigated the changes in the social climate of groups of children when under the leadership of autocratic, democratic or *laisser-faire* leaders.

Levin, Hilton and Leiderman‡ sought to find any relationship between the behaviour of teachers and the productive behaviour of their pupils. The results of this work shows that the more friendly and warm the teachers are, the more both of self-initiated and required work their pupils do.

A great deal of work has been done on the question of how teaching ability can be assessed, but the results are given mainly in terms of personal qualities and attitudes in the teacher rather than in terms of specific types of participation by the teacher when engaged in teaching.

As long ago as 1931, R. B. Cattell summarised all the work done on the subject before that date, which was by no means inconsiderable, and he then issued a questionnaire to a wide range of people in the educational world asking them to name what they considered to be the ten most important qualities of a good young teacher.

Other studies based on the collection of opinions from "experts", teachers and pupils are listed in the bibliography, as are those based on measuring the achievements and behaviour of children when in charge of different teachers — attempts to rate successful as compared with less successful teachers in terms of personality traits.

In 1951, K. M. Evans published "A critical survey of methods of assessing teaching ability."§

He mentions as the four criteria most commonly in use as (a) gain in information in pupils, (b) opinion of experts, (c) ratings on various scales, and (d) opinion of pupils. He found little agreement between the criteria and suggested that the best criterion would be a composite measure incorporating (a), (b) and (d).

---

* *Teacher–Pupil Relationships*, Macmillan, 1941.
† *Journal of Social Psychology*, Vol. X, pp. 271–299, 1939.
‡ *Journal of Experimental Education*, Vol. XXVI, 1957.
§ *British Journal of Educational Psychology*, June 1951, pp. 89–95.

Evans suggests that if one of the methods alone is more satisfactory than the others it may be (b), opinions of experts. One might have expected the opinions of teachers to be of at least equal importance, but in my own experience of analysing the interviews given by teachers whose teaching we have sampled, it became evident that most of the teachers were not consciously fully aware of the skill they were using, or probably they had become so accustomed to watching and meeting the needs of children that they had ceased to think of such behaviour as anything deserving of mention. They were more inclined to mention problems of which they had recently become aware, than their most outstanding ways of contributing to the children's progress. In this kind of investigation it may well be true that the onlooker sees more of the game.

When visiting the classrooms of good teachers one is always struck by their tendency to stand back and let the children's work be seen. The visitor will be told of the ideas suggested by the children, and success achieved by one or another child will be pointed out. Nothing will be said of their own share in bringing about a situation in which the child's ideas were accepted and used and their achievements encouraged and helped. This tendency, while it is very commendable as evidence of a teacher's unselfish interest in her pupils, sometimes misleads the inexperienced visitor who imagines that mere provision of materials and opportunities for the children have been all that was required. This preoccupation of good teachers with the children rather than themselves may explain why, when asked by research workers what they think their most important function to be, their answers reveal only a very small part of what they actually do.

It also seems very probable that the opinions of pupils might be affected by the truth that art so often *appears* to be effortless that the good teacher frequently leads the pupil to feel he has achieved success by his own efforts. I have often been told by teachers that it was only when they had had experience in schools that they came to realise that they had been well trained for teaching and still did not really understand how it had been done. They often need the experience either of meeting teachers whose training had not been so good or of having to train teachers themselves, before they are able to appraise the care and skill which had been given to their own training. If this is true of teachers who are students of education, it seems likely to be even more true of children. Even though there are undoubtedly some moments at which pupils are consciously grateful for particular acts of helpfulness and encouragement from their teachers, it seems inevitable and probably desirable that much of what is done for them escapes their conscious attention.

There seems to be still a need for studies of teachers of children of various ages, based on collected records of actual observation, which can be analysed to reveal not only the nature of qualities in the teacher, but also specific skills, the knowledge of which can be of so much help to novices in the profession as well as to those experienced teachers who are ever seeking to improve their craft.

CHAPTER III

Scope and method of conducting the enquiry

SINCE the motive for the study was largely to offer help to Infant School teachers, it was decided to focus special attention upon those aspects of the teacher's work where perplexity most often existed, i.e. a clarification, in some detail, of what good and successful teachers actually do when children of various ages are engaged in periods of freedom to choose their own activities. It was, therefore, determined that the main part of the study should consist of taking detailed records of exactly what the teacher did and, if possible, said during sample periods of 20 minutes each (i.e. a total of 180 minutes for each teacher), the samples to be recorded solely during "free choice" times. After some experiment, as described in the previous chapter, it was decided to take nine such samples from each teacher, arranging that three of the samples should be near the beginning, three in the middle and three towards the end of the time allocated to free choice. In no case were more than two samples taken on any one day, which meant that observers were doing this work on at least five different days (more frequently, six, since two samples were never taken continuously).

We were concerned to show what constitutes good and successful teaching in informal education, so care was given to the selection of teachers. Three criteria were applied. First the teachers were working in schools which on many grounds and from many people had been recommended to us as very good ones from the educational point of view. They were schools which were on a list compiled in the department as being very suitable to recommend to visitors who wished to study good progressive Infant or Nursery School methods. While there are, no doubt, many equally good and accessible schools which we have not as yet had brought to our notice, there are no schools on the list that have not been strongly recommended to us from several sources: Educational Authorities, Training Colleges for teachers whose students observe and practise in them, and last, but by no means least, the very discerning Training College lecturers, Head and assistant teachers who take our own course. Many of the schools were also personally known by myself or my colleagues and all the

Nursery Schools were also personally known by Miss Cass. I think there is, therefore, no possible doubt that the schools were those which would be generally accepted as good.

The second criterion is that of the opinion of the Headmistress, who was always asked to advise as to which teacher or teachers would be very suitable to be studied by someone wanting to watch the development week by week of the free choice period when in charge of a teacher particularly experienced and/or successful in these methods.

The third criterion was that of the judgement of the observer, who made her own final choice as to which teachers she herself would find of greatest value to study and with whom she felt a sufficient affinity to be assured that the teacher would not find her presence a strain. The observer would explain to the teacher that she would welcome the opportunity of watching an "activity period" week by week instead of only once, and would ask if the teacher would be willing to have her, going no further if any unwillingness were suggested. Since the people who volunteered for this work were those who wished for precisely the opportunity stated, there was no insincerity in this request, and though we did not want to run the risk of making the teachers self-conscious by over-stressing our interest in their own function, no teacher could be unaware that her own part in the development of the children's work would be observed. We were always prepared, if teachers commented on being rather closely watched, to say we were interested in the purposes for which children sought an adult, which was indeed a vital part of the study from its first inception. No teacher, however, did express anxiety on that score until the last year of the study when we were looking for nothing else than the purposes for which children sought the adult and, on hearing this, the teacher was at once reassured.

At that stage, one observer thought it best to tell the teacher of her main purpose, because when children crowded round the teacher it was not always possible to hear what they said and once the teachers knew of the special interest of the observer, they would tell her afterwards what each child had come for. When teachers themselves were being sampled in the earlier years, we agreed that we must run the risk of losing an occasional quietly-made comment by the teacher rather than embarrass her by following her about the room. Teacher's comments are, however, more easily audible than children's and not a great deal was lost, though the samples are not absolutely complete to the extent that the actual nature of a few very quietly-made comments to individual children were occasionally missed. It was sometimes possible to tell by the teacher's gesture or expression and the child's response that, for example, a question had been asked, praise given or a directive issued. Miss Cass had to face more formidable difficulties in that in the Nursery Schools the teacher often moved between rooms and into the garden.

Both Miss Cass and I were reassured to find that in the samples of almost every teacher there are occasional items under the category "Meditates aloud". We felt that this was an indication that the teachers were relaxed enough to behave spontaneously and that the observer had succeeded in getting herself forgotten as far as possible, which was her aim.

Observers were instructed not to begin recording the 20-minute time samples until they were sure that the teacher was thoroughly accustomed to and relaxed about the presence of the observer in the room with her. Since note-taking of various general matters was always done by observers, the more intensive note-taking during the sampling periods was not so noticeable and was done as unobtrusively as possible, observers noting points briefly and with abbreviations, to ensure accuracy, but writing them up more fully as soon as possible after leaving the school.

The careful descriptive writing up was, of course, necessary, since other observers would be co-operating in checking the analysis of the records. Without the full description involving, for example, not only what the teacher said, but how she said it, misunderstandings were sure to occur when records were analysed by observers who had not been present. For instance, a playful remark might be interpreted as "Reproof" if the observer omitted to record that it was said laughingly and with a friendly smile.

Another discipline which the observers were asked to impose upon themselves was to refrain, while in the classrooms, from making judgements or criticisms as to the desirability or otherwise of anything they saw, but to be merely observers and acceptors of the situation as they found it. It was, of course, self-evident to all the observers that to make such comments to teacher or children would affect the situation, but they were also asked to go further and not make such judgements mentally either, since facial expressions of approval or disapproval can be noted. Moreover, it is not easy to observe all there is to see if one is distracted by making judgements at the same time as observing.

Analysis of the records did, of course, involve much judgement (which had to be confirmed by other assessors) as to what was the appropriate description in general terms of each act or remark of the teachers, and later when the full eighty categories had been evolved after much experiment and discussion to decide to which category each contact should be appropriately assigned. If, after careful consideration, observers felt that no category really included

c

the episode correctly, the item was subjected to discussion by several observers. During the first year of the study (after one year of pilot work), the five observers (together with Dr. Hellman and myself) held a great many such discussions which resulted in the expansion of the number of categories to eighty (one of which was subsequently found to be unnecessary). After that stage the eighty was found to be sufficient, provided that from time to time the wording of a category was slightly broadened to admit an episode which came very near to the category as previously named, but about which there might be some slight doubt or ambiguity.

In the later years of the teacher-sampling work, a few new categories emerged, because at that time observers were working in some schools which were organised on the plan of a very informal whole day, so such categories as "Hears a child read" appeared. Since the majority of the samples obtained were taken in schools which provided definite times for the hearing of reading, this had not been an occupation of the teacher during periods of "free activity". Had a child asked to read to the teacher in one of these periods, it would no doubt have been permitted, but it did not occur; there was no record of a teacher either assenting to, refusing or postponing such a request. It therefore seemed wise to omit these episodes from the few records taken in schools with a very flexible time-table and to concentrate on the teacher's rôle when the children were receiving incidental rather than specific teaching.

To record so few of such instances would suggest that Infant teachers very seldom hear children read, and that the majority of the teachers were indifferent to the responsibility of helping the children to acquire the skills of reading, writing and arithmetic, which was certainly not true. Moreover, it is in the matter of incidental teaching when children are "playing" freely, that the most misunderstanding exists. When specific organised instruction is given, most teachers are clear about what they are going to do, though methods, of course, vary a great deal from one teacher to another. Many of the episodes which are recorded throughout the samples did, in fact, relate to the satisfaction or expansion of the child's wish to understand what books were about or to write something needed or to calculate or discover matters involving the nature of number.

As will be illustrated later in an analysis of the actual contacts made by some of the teachers, it will be seen that they cover the initiation of children into aspects of every "subject" in any primary school curriculum and sometimes beyond that, but it seemed wise to exclude episodes which related specifically to a type of time-table which was different in a few schools from that of the majority. The samples are nearly all taken from schools which devoted a definite period to "free activities" (by whatever name it was called in the various schools) whereas schools where the whole day was fluid were very few at the time our main work was in progress.

The teacher-sampling work in the Infant Schools extended over the years 1951–1958, after a pilot study in 1950–1951.

The observers who participated in this work were also asked to observe the teachers throughout the school day for at least one day and to give a general description of the school, the teacher and her work. Most of them found time to observe for more than one day. Before finally leaving the school they asked the teacher for certain information if they had not already obtained the answers by observation or informal talk with the teachers. The three matters on which we decided to try to obtain specific evidence were

(1) What links, if any, are made by the teacher between the free choice period and the rest of the curriculum provided for during the day? This question did not apply in that form to the schools with a "free day" but even in these schools we were interested to see how far the children's interests, as expressed in their spontaneous play, were taken up and used in relation to other work or whether, for example, a child would nearly always simply stop his play activities and then choose occupations unrelated to them or whether children felt a task had to be carried out before they could, in conscience, choose what they wanted to do, which idea is certainly encouraged in some schools which would claim to have a free time-table.

(2) What records, if any, were kept by the teachers? (Seeing them, if possible.)

(3) Whether discussions which related to the free choice period were held at specific times.

We wanted to enquire how far any or all of these three matters were considered to be of importance and practised by teachers who were so successful in this kind of work.

The general descriptions of the school and the teacher were asked for chiefly to throw light on the samples, and were often illuminating. For example, the teacher who most often used a device not characteristic of most of the teachers, i.e. clapping her hands to gain the children's attention, had a very soft voice and a classroom much disturbed by noise from traffic outside. The teacher whose records showed most tendency to hurry the children had to use a hall which had to be vacated at a specific time for the use of other classes.

By leaving the instructions to observers to describe the teacher and the school rather indefinite, it is not possible to say that we gathered anything like a full picture of all it would be desirable to know, but the descriptions as given have been analysed since it was thought that the most outstanding features of the teachers would not have escaped report, and many factual matters were reported on by all observers. When the time-samples had been analysed and agreed upon, charts and histograms were drawn up to reveal not only the types of contact most used by most teachers, those less used, and those which showed the greatest variation between teachers, but also differences, if any, in the type of contacts made by teachers of five-, six- and seven-year-old children respectively.

By 1958 we had obtained records of thirty teachers, ten with each of the three age-groups. We have no samples taken from an Infant teacher, taking a class of very mixed ages. In the Nursery Schools, age groups are usually mixed so it was not possible for Miss Cass to analyse her records in this particular way. I felt that, small as the numbers were, of ten teachers in each age-group, it might be suggestive and interesting to note whether teachers of younger children were using certain types of contact more or less than those of older groups and whether this threw light on the developmental needs of the children. Research on the ages of five to seven plus is not very extensive and it was possible that (however tentatively) we might be able to make suggestions which would support or perhaps amplify other findings or at least suggest avenues of further exploration.

When, in 1958, we had completed the records of thirty teachers, it seemed wise, rather than delaying the possibility of publication too long, to concentrate the time available to the observers on aspects of the work into which we felt we had not as yet penetrated sufficiently deeply. That is, on systematic interviews of a number of these and other similarly selected teachers on their own ideas of what progressive methods demanded of them, and their values and views about the difficulties, and on a much more searching enquiry into the questions mentioned above: "links", records and discussion periods. In particular, I felt it might be possible to find confirmation as to whether the differences found in teachers of different age-groups did in fact relate to the needs of children at different ages if I asked the observers in the last two years of the study to concentrate solely, and in as many classes as possible, upon the question of what led children to seek the adult.

I felt that to look more deeply into these matters might be more rewarding than to increase by a few more the numbers of teachers sampled. Especially so, since thirty teachers, together with the eighteen Nursery School teachers recorded by Miss Cass and her collaborators, constitutes a larger group of teachers than it has been found possible to study by intensive periods of recording in certain other published studies, the value of which is not in question — since intensive studies, if accumulated, can produce the kind of evidence that cannot be readily obtained by studies embracing very large numbers of subjects. At least it seems reasonable to deduce that if forty-eight successful teachers of children aged 3 to 7+ show certain characteristics in their relationships with children and their ways of teaching, there is a strong indication that these matters are of importance to success in the informal kind of teaching, and that knowledge of these findings will be suggestive and helpful to other teachers.

Miss Cass's account of her methods of procedure in the study of the eighteen Nursery School teachers is given below.

Methods of Procedure

The method eventually selected to try to find what constituted the teacher's contribution to the social climate of a group and to express this quantitatively as far as possible, was to observe and "time-sample" individual teachers, whose groups of children were felt to be, as judged by several experienced people, happy and secure.

The teachers were chosen because they appeared to be understanding and sensitive to children's needs, able to give and receive affection, provide a rich environment, and to have had sufficient experience to give them confidence in their own judgements. No teacher in her first year out of College was selected, although those chosen differed in age, length of training and experience.

Harold H. Anderson and Helen and J. M. Brewer of Illinois in their book *Teacher's Classroom Personalities*, state that they had found that records of 300 minutes to 400 minutes of observation, appeared to give a generally reliable picture of an individual teacher's personality. Therefore, in our observations of the eighteen Nursery School teachers we were able to select, it was decided to record as much as possible of what they said and did for 75 minutes on each of four days.

A preliminary visit lasting for a whole morning, was paid, in order that the observer might become familiar with the general pattern and routine of the group, the building and equipment available, and the teacher's voice and manner.

There were, of course, a number of practical difficulties which arose. It was essential that the teacher herself was untroubled by what was taking place, that she was not, in fact, aware that what she said and did with the children was being recorded. One or two teachers did actually discover that they were being observed, but they were confident, secure people and it did not really worry them.

The Nursery School teacher, too, is also rarely in one place for any length of time. She moves freely from playroom to garden, from cloakroom to toilet or corridor, and to follow her without arousing her anxieties or getting in her way, and to hear all that she said was obviously out of the question. Nor was it always possible either, to see, hear or record what was involved in the inflection of a voice, the expression on a face, the movement of a hand or a spontaneous gesture, or any of those indefinable contacts which make up the personality of an individual and which must, therefore, have their effect upon children. Ideally too, it would have been good to have been able to protect these selected teachers from distractions and interruptions which prevented them from giving their full attention to their children. However, this was a reality situation and the hazards involved by the occasional absence of a helper, or the time taken up by the appearance of the school nurse, or a visitor had to be accepted. It happened to all of the teachers observed at one time or another.

It would have been interesting to have made some of the observations during the mid-day meal, or in story or music time. It was felt, however, that the play period would be the most fruitful and satisfactory, so all the observations were made then. It is easy to recognise the importance of the teacher at times when she has gathered children together for some specific activity, to tell them a story, to provide music for them to sing or move to, to serve their mid-day meal and preside at the lunch table. The play period, however, is often less easily recognised as a time when the rôle of the teacher is of the utmost importance and when all her skill is needed in guiding, enriching and providing for the all-round growth, needs and experiences of the children in her care.

All the teachers were working in well-equipped playrooms, generally with "family" groupings, i.e. children from two to five years of age, though the proportion of two-year-old children was very small and in some groups there were none at all. The size of the group varied somewhat, depending on the daily attendance, but it was generally between twenty to twenty-five, and the time of year when the observations were made also varied somewhat from teacher to teacher.

The classification of contacts in the time samples made in analysing the teachers' remarks and approaches to the children were those selected in the first year of the study. To these observations certain additions were made as they were found to occur during subsequent observations. Those which proved to be most significant were those which were observed from the beginning. It will be noted that some of these contacts relate to more than one situation, e.g. a teacher may give affection, comfort, etc. In the examples given, however, it should be clear as to which specific situation they refer, though the actual interpretation of what it signified to the child is much more subtle and less easy to define. It is often difficult, for example, to distinguish between "giving help" and "showing care for comfort", between "asking help" and "contributing an interest", by "making a suggestion" or "giving a command".

One really needs to know the children very well indeed to be able to decide whether in fact a contact was "a giving" or "a taking away". Help at one moment to one child might be a gift, the building up of a relationship, but for another child the withholding of help might be an assumption of the ability to be independent, and might therefore be the more positive approach, though less obvious as such to the observer. The impinging of one contact on another, the categories chosen, the actual order in which they have been placed and their interpretation are, of course, open to question. At the moment of impact when the observer put her contact into a particular category, added another, and interpreted it in a particular way, it seemed the right thing to do. When all the material had been assembled I worked over it again and as a result have combined one or two of the original categories where overlap was particularly extensive. Otherwise I judged it to be wiser to leave the original categories unchanged as despite some inevitable overlap they seemed, on the whole, to represent different aspects of the Nursery School teachers' ways of helping the children.

CHAPTER IV

Results of the analysis of the records

IN reporting these I have grouped the findings according to what appears to be the most important motive behind the actions of the teachers, as this seemed more likely to be of interest to the reader, than to have presented merely a long list of separate items. The original order of items was merely based on the order in which episodes occurred and not on a preconceived scheme, since our main concern was to show what teachers actually did and not to make judgements at the time of recording.

The classification adopted now for the purpose of coherent reporting is as follows:

I. Those actions of the teacher which show concern with the provision of intellectual stimulus or imparting knowledge. I have used two sub-headings, i.e.:

IA. Episodes in which the teacher communicates more directly and personally with the children.

IB. Those where the material environment is used to assist in giving knowledge and experience.

II. Actions of the teacher which particularly show concern with fostering and encouraging good social attitudes.

These are arranged under three sub-headings, following an order which seems a logical sequence, since before it would be rewarding to expect children to co-operate well with the teacher or with other children they need to be assured of protection and comfort and the affection of the adult. The sub-headings therefore are:

IIA. Actions rendering personal care, protection or comfort.

IIB. Personal friendly advances from teacher to child.

IIC. Direct attempts to promote social attitudes in the children.

Group III consists of ways in which the teacher establishes a general setting which is favourable to education and which are of equal importance to the child's emotional, social and intellectual welfare.

Sub-headings are as follows:

IIIA. Observation of the children.

IIIB. Praise and encouragement.

IIIC. Discipline and control.

The last group, IV, is of less importance but must be included in order to complete the picture of the way in which the teachers were engaged. It consists of the actions of teachers which did not entail direct contact with the children in their own classes.

There is inevitably overlap between the groups, but categories have been assigned to the class to which they appear most particularly to relate. One would not, of course, deny for instance, that there is much learning involved in co-operating with other people, or much discipline in the mastering of intellectual problems and difficulties, and one could give countless other instances of overlap. The teachers clearly made no hard and fast classification of their own motives and actions. They are merely reported in this way to give some sense of coherence to the reader and to show where the balance of the teacher's contribution is heavier or lighter and whether or not it varies in teachers of younger or older children.

I have given very careful consideration to the question as to whether it would be possible to bring Miss Cass's results of the Nursery School teachers into exact relationship with mine on the Infant School teachers, but there are various reasons why it is not generally practicable to do so. The two studies were originally undertaken quite separately and in the Nursery School study broader categories were used which involve more than one of the Infant School's more detailed categories. Certain categories apply only to the Nursery School and relate to some extent to the different conditions and staffing of Nursery Schools. It seemed best, therefore, to report the Nursery School results separately, but, wherever it happens that a category is precisely or very nearly the same as an Infant School category, to bring the total numbers of the Nursery School records into proportionate relationship with the Infant School records, thereby making comparison for the different age-groups possible. This meant reducing considerably the total number of Nursery School episodes, since the Nursery School teachers were observed on four days each only but over periods of 75 minutes on each day, thus giving a total of 300 minutes, whereas the Infant teachers were observed on nine different occasions but for spans of 20 minutes, which gives a total of 180 minutes only. Moreover, there were eighteen Nursery School teachers as compared with ten teachers in each of the three Infant School age-groups.

It must, however, be emphasised that the Nursery School records cannot be as complete as those of the Infant School, for the reasons given by Miss Cass. The Nursery School teacher moves frequently between garden, classroom and cloakroom which she is enabled to do by the presence of Nursery assistants, whereas the Infant School teacher with no such additional help must on the whole for most of the time remain with the majority of her class. It was agreed that observers should not follow the teacher about, since this would have caused a very unnatural relationship and have spoilt the spontaneity of the teacher's relations with the children, therefore it was inevitable that a higher proportion of the Nursery School teachers' actions escaped the observers and could not be recorded. Wherever, therefore, I have compared proportional figures as between Nursery and Infant teachers it should be noted that the Nursery *actual* number of episodes were almost certainly considerably higher — if, for example, the Nursery teachers come only slightly below those of teachers of five-year-olds, they were in fact probably above them.

FULL TABLE OF CONTACTS MADE BY THE TEACHER
INFANT SCHOOL STUDY

Group IA	Actions of the teacher which show concern with the provision of intellectual stimulus or the imparting of information.	Total no. of contacts
No. 1	Questions child (or children's actions or activities) to obtain information which the teacher wishes to know, in order to understand a situation and thus know what help if any may be needed or to check that the child is getting correct information or using appropriate aids.	1260
No. 2	Helps by giving information or explanation spontaneously.	1230
No. 3	Remarks made with the sole object of stimulating to further activity.	574
No. 4	Helps by questioning a child to help him towards the solution of a problem or towards gaining further information.	549
No. 5	Helps by drawing the child's attention to something relevant.	327
No. 6	Helps by giving information or explanation in answer to children's questions.	307
No. 7	Helps by demonstrating a skill.	258
No. 8	Repeats a child's statement, answer or question in order to check on what the child has actually said, to make it clear to others, or to make clear what help is needed.	110
No. 9	Rejects a suggestion.	108
No. 10	Corrects a child's work or speech.	85
No. 11	Teacher admits lack of knowledge.	2
No. 12	Teacher admits lack of knowledge but undertakes to find out.	1

Group IB	Actions of the teacher where the material environment is used to assist in giving knowledge and experience.	
No. 13	Helps by producing material.	489
No. 14	The teacher herself attends to the care of material and equipment.	460
No. 15	Helps by directing the use of material.	285
No. 16	Helps by indicating the whereabouts of material.	254
No. 17	Helps by rendering assistance in the management of materials.	252
No. 18	Attends herself to the management of classroom materials.	185
No. 19	Helps by suggesting the use of material.	147

Group IIA	Actions of rendering physical care, protection or comfort.	

No. 20	Helps by attending to child's clothing or physical comfort.	189
No. 21	Comforts and reassures by speaking to a child.	218
No. 22	Comforts or reassures by caress.	67

Group IIB	Personal friendly advances from teacher to child.	

No. 23	Chats to a child.	593
No. 24	Makes friendly gestures other than those needed for comfort.	515
No. 25	Makes a promise to a child.	116
No. 26	Plays with child by joining in spontaneously.	71
No. 27	Greets a child.	54
No. 28	Laughs with a child.	50
No. 29	Friendly laughing at a child, but not in mockery.	44
No. 30	Plays with child by accepting an invitation to join in an activity.	20
No. 31	Plays with child by asking to join in activity.	2

Group IIc	Actions of the teacher which show concern with promoting social attitudes (i) by direct means and (ii) by example.	

(i)

No. 32	Requests the child's help or co-operation.	577
No. 33	Enlists co-operation between the child and herself.	255
No. 34	Promotes social attitudes between children or considerate behaviour.	151
No. 35	Directs or encourages the children to co-operate.	102
No. 36	Enlists co-operation between children.	96
No. 37	Arbitrates.	39
No. 38	Provides an audience by suggesting that other children shall watch	10
No. 39	Takes verbal action to protect a child.	10
No. 40	Takes physical action to protect a child.	1
No. 41	Rejects an offer of help.	5

(ii) (By example)

No. 42	Thanks a child.	190
No. 43	Asks a child's permission.	26

Group IIIA Observations of the children.

No. 44	Observes children without commenting.	522
No. 45	Observes material or child's work without commenting.	185
No. 46	Provides audience by watching an individual child.	71
No. 47	Provides audience by watching a group of children.	35

Negative

No. 48	Ignores child because not noticed.	8

Group IIIB Praise and encouragement.

No. 49	Assents by word or gesture.	920
No. 50	Praises child's performance, work or action.	851
No. 51	Stimulates by encouragement.	333
No. 52	Helps by doing part of the child's work for him.	254
No. 53	Praises child's gift.	63
No. 54	Praises child's possessions.	54
No. 55	Praises child's help.	38
No. 56	Praises child's appearance.	20

Group IIIc Actions of the teacher which are concerned with maintaining discipline and control of the children's behaviour.

No. 57	Suggests or advises appropriate action or behaviour.	912
No. 58	Gives a positive command.	836
No. 59	Arrests attention by speaking to the children.	220
No. 60	Disapproves or discourages an action by words.	166
No. 61	Disciplines by reproof.	145
No. 62	Gives a warning that it is nearly time to clear up.	79
No. 63	Stimulates by reproof.	68

No. 64	Stimulates children by telling them to hurry.	66
No. 65	Arrests attention by clapping hands.	39
No. 66	Disciplines by her own example.	35
No. 67	Disciplines by isolating a child from others.	26
No. 68	Stimulates by comparison.	21
No. 69	Arrests attention by asking children to show their hands or some similar direction.	12
No. 70	Arrests attention by signals previously agreed upon with the children.	12
No. 71	Shows disapproval by impatient movements.	10
No. 72	Disciplines by depriving the child of toys, tools, etc.	7
No. 73	Disapproves by glance or gesture.	6
No. 74	Arrests attention by raising voice.	2
No. 75	Ignores child deliberately.	1

Group IV	Actions of teachers when not in direct contact with the children of their own classes.

No. 76	Chats to other adults or visitors including children from other classes.	366
No. 77	Withdraws if necessary to attend to other business or other children.	281
No. 78	Attends to administration.	252
No. 79	Meditates aloud.	113

NURSERY SCHOOL STUDY

GROUP IA (Concerned with intellectual stimulus or the imparting of information).	Total no. of contacts
No. 1	Contributes categorical information, provides intellectual information and ideas, confirms and invites confirmation of information from the child.	1560
No. 2	Invites spontaneous information and ideas from the child.	891
No. 3	Clarifies a situation by explanation, explains the nature of materials, her own activities and the reasons for her questions, requests, refusals and actions.	828
No. 4	Spontaneously offers help, materials, permission or information.	513

No. 5	Stimulates the child's interest or draws the child's attention to something new.	276
No. 6	Corrects child's information, speech or manners.	157
No. 7	Questions child to help him solve a problem.	146
No. 8	Questions or comments on the child's ideas, information or material.	89

Group Iʙ (Concerned with material).

No. 9	Reminds the child of the use and care of equipment.	6

Group IIᴀ (Physical care, protection and comfort).

No. 10	Gives affection, comfort, personal attention or assurance.	519
No. 11	Warns the child of danger.	185
No. 12	Suggests that the child ask help from his mother.	4

Group IIʙ (Personal friendly advances).

No. 13	Grants immediately the child's request for help, objects, attention or permission.	535
No. 14	Shows admiration for or interest in a child's clothes, possessions or productions or confidence in the child's relatives or interest in his home life.	533
No. 15	Shares child's feelings and imaginative play, laughter, talks or jokes.	361
No. 16	Greets or draws a child into a social situation.	207
No. 17	Shows pleasure in child's presence or interest in his personal condition.	156
No. 18	Unspoken friendly contacts.	7

Group IIc (Promoting social attitudes).

(i) by direct means

No. 19	Asks or invites a child's help or co-operation, or draws attention to the child's ability to help himself.	773

No. 20 Contacts likely to promote a good social attitude or an increase in social awareness by any of the following means:

By recognising or promoting co-operation.
By suggesting that one child offers or gives, asks or accepts help from another.
By suggesting that one child invites another to play with him.
By pointing out the discomfort of one child to another.
By reminding children that others have feelings.   695

No. 21 Demands a child's help or co-operation.   178

No. 22 Agrees to grant requests for objects, help or permission after postponement.   149

No. 23 Thanks a child for help or gift.   145

No. 24 Arbitrates in a dispute.   123

No. 25 Refuses child's help, gift or production.   39

No. 26 Accepts the child's help or gifts.   37

(ii) by example

No. 27 Apologises to child.   34

No. 28 Asks child's permission.   1

Group IIIA (Observes children).

This was not separately recorded.

Group IIIB (Praise and encouragement).

No. 29 Accepts a child's information and ideas.   717

No. 30 Encourages the child by admiration or approval of an achievement or production.   334

No. 31 Encourages child by suggestion.   281

No. 32 Commends child's behaviour.   132

No. 33 Encourages by reassurance.   110

Group IIIc (Discipline and control).

No. 34 Reminds child of routine activity.   441

No. 35 Gives a child a specific order.   399

No. 36	Reproaches child for behaviour, untidiness or noise.	229
No. 37	Refuses or deflects child's request for help, objects, attention or permission.	146
No. 38	Checks child's activity.	20
No. 39	Ignores child's remark or action.	19
No. 40	Rejects, suggests or reminds child of an acceptable form of behaviour.	5

Group IV (When not in direct contact with children in her class).

No. 41	Meditates aloud.	155
No. 42	Seeks adult co-operation, asks or gives information to adult.	27
No. 43	Mentions child to adult in child's presence.	18
No. 44	Mentions child to adult in the hearing of other children.	15
No. 45	Exclamations used by the teacher.	10

GROUP IA

Actions of the teacher which show concern with the provision of intellectual stimulus or the imparting of information

For the sake of clarity the results within each group are given in order of the frequency of their occurrence in the study of the Infant teachers. Comments will be made to show where the addition of the records of the Nursery School teachers would have altered the order. The results of the study of the Nursery School teachers will always follow those of the Infant School study. In many cases the broader groupings of the Nursery School study provide an interesting amplification of the data first presented in the more detailed form of classification used for the work on the Infant School teachers.*

In the records of the Infant School teachers, two categories come very close together having scored respectively total numbers of 1260

* For histogram showing the total number of contacts in group Ia and group b., see page 123.

D

and 1230 contacts over the nine periods of observation from the sample records of the thirty teachers.

There are:

No. 1. "Questions child (or children's actions or activities) to obtain information which the teacher wishes to know, in order to understand a situation and thus know what help if any may be needed or to check that the child is getting correct information or using appropriate aids.

This contact is used by every teacher but shows some fairly marked variation as to how much it is used by different teachers. Averages, however, are high. Teachers of six- and seven-year-old children, however, use it considerably more. Averages are 29 for teachers of five-year-olds, are 49 for teachers of six-year-olds and 47 for those of seven-year-olds. This contact is one of several in Group I which show a steep rise from teachers of five-year-olds to those of children over six and makes an interesting suggestion that the sensitive Infant teacher is aware of how much the child over six is concerned with gaining specific knowledge and skill. The lower number of these contacts with the teachers of five-year-olds should perhaps however be seen against the record "Observes children without commenting" where they score higher than teachers of six-year-olds.

NURSERY SCHOOL STUDY

The contact which comes nearest to the above is probably N.8*,

* The Nursery School contacts have been listed as N.1, N.2, etc., to differentiate them from those of the Infant School study.

"Questions or comments on child's ideas, information or material", but since this category includes the word "comments" and does not specify the particular motives of the teacher when asking questions it does not seem profitable to bring it into close relationship with the above. It is the lowest in the table of Nursery School teachers contacts in Group I and since, even with the additional "comments" the total number of those contacts is proportionately decidedly lower than those of the teachers of five-year-old children it perhaps supports the suggestion made above that teachers of younger children may use this means of helping the children less than other means and less than of teachers of children over six.

GENERAL COMMENT

The use of this contact by all the teachers and in particular by teachers of children over six emphasises the importance attached by good teachers to the need to co-operate closely with the ideas and plans of the children. They evidently find many situations where they do not think it advisable to offer help before ascertaining what these are. However, as is shown by the almost equal numbers of contacts in the category which follows it is also clear that they find many other occasions when they do not need to ask questions to be sure that their contribution will be useful or at least worth offering.

EXAMPLES OF NO. 1

Teacher: "Who made the plan?"
Child: "I'm the planner."
Teacher: "And who are you Geoffrey?"
Another child: "I'm the chief."
Teacher: "And what are you doing Leonard?"
Geoffrey: "I'm one of the workmen."

(To child studying an Atlas) "What place are you looking for?"

"Betty, are you going by the recipe?"

Teacher (in response to child's request for material): "What do you want it for?"
Child: "To make a roof for my house?"
(Teacher finds suitable material for the child's purpose.)

"Well, do Jimmy and George know what they want to do?"

"How much money have you taken today?"

"Who is going to make the telephone kiosk? Did anyone decide?"

No. 2. "Helps by giving information or explanation spontaneously."

Again this category is used by all thirty teachers and, as in No. 1, there is considerable variation between teachers.

Average scores are 36, 47 and 41.

Girl brings a jar half full of water.
Teacher: "You will need more water than that, dear. The stems won't reach the water and the flowers won't get a drink."

Teacher (in response to child looking puzzled): "The stones are heavy so they sink. Cork is light, that's why it floats."

"It (i.e. the pastry) has to be stiff for scones. You have to roll it."

NURSERY SCHOOL STUDY

Again there is only a partial overlap between the Nursery School and Infant School categories. Category N.4 stresses both spontaneity and the giving of help to the child's learning — it reads "Spontaneously offers help, materials, permission, information", whereas the Infant No. 2 is limited to information or explanation. Mention must also be made of another Category (N.1) which, though its wording is designed to separate the purely spontaneous remarks of the teacher from the more conscious and deliberate attempts to teach, has an undoubted overlap with the Infant School No. 2. N.1, "Contributes categorical information, provides intellectual information and ideas, confirms and invites confirmation from the child."

This has the highest single score over all the Nursery School separate categories and serves to show that good teachers, even of the youngest children, in no way underestimate their rôle in regard to actual teaching. The total number of contacts under category N.1 as always given proportionately to the Infant records, is 520, as against the total score of 144 for teachers of five-year-olds and the number of N.4 which is somewhat nearer to No. 2 (Infant School) is 171 which, if added, would bring the Nursery School teachers above the teachers of five-year-olds to a high degree. Since, however, both categories embrace a wider range of contacts it is not possible to use these figures to show whether the Nursery School teachers are higher or lower in this particular aspect of their contact with the children than teachers of any other age-group. It is, however, clearly evident that the Nursery School teachers are doing a very considerable amount of actual teaching.

It may be that the assistance of helpers enables the Nursery School eacher to give a higher proportion of her time to specifically 'teaching" contacts, whereas the teacher of five-year-olds has to divide her time more often between these and contacts related to giving physical care to children.

The next two categories also come very near to each other with total scores of 574 for No. 3 and 549 for No. 4.

No. 3. "Remarks made with the sole object of stimulating to further activity."

This category includes the remarks made by teachers which open up to the child fresh possibilities of developing his activity further than he had thought of. It was not a matter merely of encouragement. When encouragement or praise only was used it has been listed separately. Reminders to the child of goals which he had intended but of which he had lost sight would be included. Most of such remarks did of course have the effect of encouraging the child as did many other acts and deeds of the teacher. For that reason I have adopted the narrower word, "Praise", to indicate these contacts where verbal commendation of the child's efforts and achievements are the sole stimuli used." These are of great importance but are reported under Group III since they are not directly concerned with adding to the child's knowledge but rather to help in the establishment of an atmosphere and relationship with the teacher which releases the child's own efforts and capacity for achievement.

No. 3 occurs in the records of twenty-nine of the thirty teachers. Teachers of six-year-olds fluctuate more than those of seven-year-olds where no teacher has less than 12 such contacts. Averages show a fairly steady rise from 5 to 7 with (unlike most of the other categories in this group) a rather steeper rise between six and seven than that between five and six.

The averages are 15 per teacher of five-year-olds.

     18 ,, ,, ,, six-year-olds.
     25 ,, ,, ,, seven-year-olds.

EXAMPLES OF NO. 3

"I should show him your plan, then you can organise your workmen and start making the hall."

"Good, bring your doll along and some wool and pins and we'll see what we can do." (To child who said she'd like to knit a frock for her doll.)

"Perhaps you could read it in the hall after prayers."

Child: "If we build it any higher, won't it fall over?"
Teacher: "Shall we see?"

"Add up your scores and see who has the highest score."

"Betty, would you like to see if you can find some different shaped leaves in the garden, narrow ones, short ones."

"That's very nice, dear, would you like to put another design in the spaces?"

NURSERY SCHOOL STUDY

Here we have a category N.5 "Stimulates the child's interest or draws the child's attention to something new" which comes very close to No. 3 of the Infant School study. The proportionate number of contacts is 93 which brings the Nursery School teachers below the scores of the teachers of five and six, and still more of course below the seven-year-olds. Moreover, some allowance should probably be made for the phrase "Draws the child's attention to something new" which is an important part of the work of a Nursery School teacher when introducing very young children to a rich and unfamiliar environment. The need for this contact is possibly less for teachers of older children since, owing to the children's greater experience, fewer objects are unfamiliar and therefore when new objects come into the classroom they would probably be quickly noted and remarked on so that it would not often be necessary for teachers to draw the attention of children to new things. The category described below, "Draws the child's attention to something relevant", does not exclude the possibility that it might at times be something new, but more often it was the possibilities of using, thinking about or comparing with something in a new way rather than that the object was new.

No. 4. "Helps by questioning a child to help him towards the solution of a problem or towards gaining further information."

This contact appears in the sampled records of twenty-eight of the teachers. The two whose records do not include it are both teachers of five-year-olds. It is clear throughout that this was a contact less used by the teachers of five-year-olds as a whole, averages rise steeply from 11 for teachers of five-year-olds to 20 and 22 respectively in the other two groups.

EXAMPLES OF NO. 4

Boy is making a roundabout but cannot fix the central pole.
Teacher: "If you just put the pole through what will happen?"
Child: "It will fall over."
Teacher: "What do you want at the bottom?"

Child (who has made some tickets): "What shall I put on them?"
Teacher: "What do you have on tickets, dear?"

"How many inches is it right across your shield?"
"Now we must find the middle—what is it?"

"How much do you think it weighs? How much were you short?"

"There isn't any orange paint left. I wonder how we can make some orange paint?"

Child: "I want a flag to put on top of this castle."
Teacher: "What sort? Is it British, French, German? What sort of castle is it?"

Boy: "Shall I use blue or black?"
Teacher: "Now what would look better against the blue?"

NURSERY SCHOOL STUDY

N.7, "Questions child to help him solve a problem", is clearly very close to the above. The proportionate score for this contact is 49, which brings it below the five-year-old records and seems to support the suggestion that promoting reasoning by the method of questioning younger children, though used at times by nearly all teachers, is not found to be generally as fruitful as when applied to older Infant School children which is to be expected in view of what we know about the best reasoning of the young child being so much in relation to first-hand experience. Whether the teachers are influenced by this as a psychological principle or merely that they have discovered it to be so one cannot tell. Certainly they appear to rely more on other means of getting the child thinking and learning.

Categories 5, 6 and 7 have total scores of 327, 307, and 258.

No. 5. "Helps by drawing the child's attention to something relevant."

This contact is used less by the teachers of five-year-old children. There is considerable variation as between different teachers but on the whole it is used a good deal by teachers in the upper Infant School. Averages are 5, 14 and 13.

This category does not appear in the Nursery School records.

EXAMPLES OF No. 5

"Come and have a look at this picture?" (To help a child in difficulties over making a model.)

"I don't think we've got any sugar. Look at the recipe book and see if there is one without any sugar."

"We'll see what is in the junk box. Maybe there is something suitable there."

"Have a look at the railway book." (To a child who wanted to make a platform.)

Boy making out a bill writes 12*d*.
Teacher: "Just a minute. The man in the shop wouldn't say 12*d*. What would he say?"
Boy: "Oh, a shilling."
Teacher: 'Yes, a shilling, so change your pennies into shillings whenever you have twelve."

No. 6. "Helps by giving information or explanation in answer to children's questions."

Except for one teacher who answered questions 41 times during the nine sampling periods, the teachers of five-year-olds do less answering than do the teachers of the older age-groups. Averages are 7 (five-year-olds), 13 (six-year-olds) and 11 (seven-year-olds). One teacher of five- and one of seven-year-olds does not score at all. Over the group as a whole there is plenty of indication that teachers are generous about responding to the questions of the children and aware of the value of doing so as a means of giving fresh knowledge and understanding since, as will be seen later, there are very few instances, in the Infant School study, of teachers ignoring a child it must be that the scores in this category relate to the number of questions asked by the children of the teacher. However, it is possible that some teachers encourage children to ask more than others.

Nursery School Study

The answering of questions is not separately recorded in this study but is embraced under the wider heading of N.1 which emphasises the teacher's contributions of contributing information and of confirming information from the child. While this would include some answering of children's factual questions, since this has not been recorded separately it is not possible to relate it to the Infant School study.

Examples of No. 6 (Infant School Study)

Child: "I use this don't I?"
Teacher: "Yes, that's the tool to use. It's name is the brace and bit. Can you fix it together?"

Child: "What sort of dog is that?"
Teacher: "It's a poodle, Deborah, and it is called 'Jet' because it's all black."

Boy, reading a letter, asks the teacher what two of the words say and she tells him.

Boy (making a clay plaque): "What shall I do now?"
Teacher gives directions.

No. 7. "Helps by demonstrating a skill."

This record is the first to show less striking differences between teachers than the other categories so far cited. Only two teachers have no recorded instance of it (both teachers of five-year-olds). Averages of the teachers of five- and seven-year-olds are both 10. The average falls to 6 with teachers of six-year-olds. On the whole the evidence shows that, while this method of teaching is widely used and to a considerable degree, it is not one of the methods used most. No teacher's record is as high as it is in several cases in the other categories so far listed. The drop at six years old will be referred to later with reference to other categories in which teachers of six-year-olds rise above or fall below the averages of both the teachers of younger and of older children. While no single item on numbers as small as this can be claimed as a result which cannot be ascribed to chance factors or to the particular characteristics of certain individual teachers it is at least suggestive when one finds a consistency in certain allied items, that this reflects something of the special characteristics of six-year-olds, and in other categories also which involved the use by the teacher of material, the averages are lower with six-year-olds.

One might at least ask the question, "Is it possible that the six-year-old who is by now familiar with the school equipment and general management of materials such as clay and paint but has not yet reached the stage of criticising his products from the criterion of reality and therefore, wishing for more definite skill, is less in need of demonstration either than the five-year-olds or the seven?"

Nursery School Study

This item does not appear among the categories listed. It is, of course, well known that very young children are seldom prepared to watch anything as formal as a "demonstration". Items in batteries of mental tests which require the child of Nursery School age to watch and then repeat a performance are difficult to administer since the child's impulse is to experiment and not to watch. It is probable, however, that some very informal demonstration took place accompanying, for example, such items as in N.3, "Explains the nature of materials", and N.5, "Stimulates the child's interest and draws the child's attention to something new." The word "demonstrates" is probably too formal to be appropriate here.

Examples of No. 7 (Infant School Study)

Child: "That's number 1."
Teacher: "Yes, that's right. Shall we write it?" (She proceeds to write number 1 on the page.) "This is the corner we put the number in."

"You want it about three inches square. Three inches that way" (shows the child how to place the ruler). "Do you see?"

Child: "Our dough is too wet."
Teacher: "Is it?" (She picks up flour sifter and sprinkles it on the dough—then kneads the dough.) "If you keep it well floured it won't stick to the board."

Child (making a handkerchief): "What do I do now?"
Teacher takes material and demonstrates how to turn in one raw edge to make a hem. "Now you do that to the other three edges."

Child: "Can I have a handle to put on my calendar?"
Teacher finds ribbon and says: "How do you want it put on? Like that?" (She demonstrates.)

Categories 8, 9 and 10 have considerably smaller numbers of instances than those so far described and come close together. Their order may well be due to chance factors as indeed is the case with any of the items which I have grouped together because of their proximity. The total number of contacts are as follows: 110, 108 and 85. Small numbers, however, in samples of only nine periods of 20 minutes each are not to be ignored since they clearly represent part of the techniques of the teachers concerned and would almost certainly have occurred much more frequently had it been possible to take more records for longer periods. It would, however, be correct to say that the use of these techniques tends to be considerably less than those cited above.

No. 8. "Repeats a child's statement, answer or question in order to check on what the child has actually said, to make it clear to others, or to make clear what help is needed."

This ties up rather closely with No. 1 and perhaps serves to support No. 1 as being the most widely used of all the categories. It is another way of the teacher making sure that she is fully in touch with the child's mind and is a strong characteristic of all good educators.

Some teachers who are high in No. 1 are low here and it seems evident that some teachers prefer asking questions to achieve the same need of clarification of the child's ideas.

Some teachers have a habit of echoing a child's words partly in sympathy and encouragement and it is doubtful whether the interpretation of this category is wholly appropriate to every incident recorded under it, though it appears to be the main motive behind most of the repetitions. The addition of the words "Or in sympathy to reassure the child that his meaning has been heard and accepted" might have been a desirable addition to the name of this category. It is one of the instances where interpretation of the purpose of the contact was not always easy and it was originally merely called "Repeats a child's statement." It is not listed in the Nursery School study.

EXAMPLES OF NO. 8

Child: "It makes 1/1½d."
Teacher: "Yours makes 1/1½d.—I wonder if that is right—I'll come and see."

Child: "Fifteen minutes."
Teacher: "Yes, fifteen minutes."

Teacher: "What would happen if the car was too big?"
Child: "It wouldn't go in the garage."
Teacher (smiling): "No, it wouldn't go inside the garage, would it?"

Child (showing a picture): "It's a Slumberland mattress."
Teacher (puzzled): "A Slumberland mattress? What is a Slumberland mattress?"
Boy: "A big lorry."
Teacher: "Oh, I know what you mean. You mean a big van with Slumberland mattresses inside."

Boy: "It's going to have two strong what's-her-names to hold it up."
Teacher (laughing): "What's 'what's-her-names'?"
Boy: "Two bits of wood."
(Both laugh and teacher then supplies the name the boy wanted.)

No. 9. "Rejects a suggestion."

This, though rather a negative way of teaching, which one is not surprised to find falling rather low in the records of these good teachers, can, however, be a necessary aid to learning and was often accompanied by an explanation so that the rejection of the suggestion did not imply rejection of the child. Five teachers have no entry. Averages are 2, 5 and 4 for the groups in chronological order. Again there is no separate record in the Nursery School study though it probably occurs occasionally under N.8, "Questions or comments on child's ideas, information or material."

EXAMPLES OF NO. 9

Child (calling from cooking table): "Shall I put another bottle of milk in?"
Teacher: "Not a whole bottle, a half."

Child: "Will you make this into a loom for me?"
Teacher: "It's too thin, this is much better."

Child: "Can I do some knitting?"
Teacher: "There's not enough time now, dear."

Child: "He's pinched my needle."
Teacher: "No he hasn't—look, Maureen, it's on the floor, you dropped it."

Child: "Can you put some brown powder in this jar?"
Teacher: "No, I don't want to put any new paint in because I want to get all the jars washed out this afternoon. Isn't there another jar?"

No. 10. "Corrects a child's work or speech."

All teachers of seven-year-olds have some records of doing this but there are four teachers in each of the other age-groups who have none. Averages are 2, 2 and 5 in chronological order. Again one is prompted to ask a very tentative question, "Does this tie up at all with the seven-year-olds' greater concern with skill and with standards based on reality?" It might, of course, reflect the teachers' feelings that now the child is older he ought to get speech more correct and work with greater accuracy — or again it might be due merely to a chance factor that the teachers in the seven-year-old classes happened to be ones who were rather more concerned about accuracy in the performance of the children.

EXAMPLES OF NO. 10

"No, that's not the 4 oz. weight."

Child (counting dinner money): "There's 4/5*d*."
Teacher: "There should be 4/6*d*. Let me check it." (Counts and reveals that one pile which should be of 12 pennies has 13.) "Look Peter, 11, 12, 13."

Child: "I wanted to do it careful."
Teacher: "Carefully—yes, you've done it very carefully."

Boy: "Can I borrow a tape measure?"
Teacher: "Do you mean a ruler, old chap?"
Boy: "Yes."

NURSERY SCHOOL STUDY

N.6 is "Corrects a child information, speech or manners". The addition of the word "Manners" makes it doubtful whether this category should be recorded under "Discipline" or "Direct attempts to promote social attitudes". Since, however, the first two matters are clearly concerned with acquiring knowledge and also since at this early age "manners" is so largely a case of the child being taught what is acceptable behaviour in the eyes of the adult, it seemed appropriate to place it here though in comparison with the Infant School study numbers may need to be slightly discounted on the grounds that correction of manners is not recorded in No. 10. The Nursery School proportional score is 52 which is higher than the teachers of five- and six-year-olds and equal to those of seven-year-olds. It should perhaps also be noted that "Information" is not the same as "work" and while it is very improbable that these young children would do much "work" that needed correction (and, indeed, apparatus of the more didactic kind is usually self-corrective) it is an age when there are many confusions and misunderstandings about the phenomenon of the outer world and when children often need help in sorting out fact from fantasy.

The last two categories, Nos. 11 and 12, have records so small as to be almost negligible except that it should be recorded that the episodes did occur.

No. 11. "Teacher admits lack of knowledge."

Has two entries only — one of which, moreover, is very dubious since it is merely "I don't know" in response to a child's question as to what colour he should use for painting an object in his picture and implies not lack of knowledge so much as a wish to throw the child on his own resources.

No. 12. "Admits lack of knowledge but undertakes to find out."

Has one episode only from a teacher of seven-year-olds. The almost total absence of records under these two headings is surprising when one considers how much children tend to ask when pursuing their genuine purposes and interests. The observers commented on this and said they thought it tied up with the fact that nearly all these records were taken in schools where there was a definite period for free choice, often of not longer than an hour, and discussion periods were taken at another time and not recorded here. In schools with a free time-table and consequently greater leisure for teachers and children during periods of free creative work there is no doubt questions do arise which send teachers and often children to reference books. Had all these observations been conducted in schools of that kind it is probable that more such incidents would have occurred in the records. There is no specific heading for these categories in the Nursery School study.

The two incidences were:

No. 11

Child: "Will this colour do?"
Teacher: "I don't know—just try it."

No. 12

Child (showing a tea packet): "I looked in my larder, but I couldn't find out where that came from."
Teacher: "I don't know either, but I can find out for you."

SPECIAL NOTE ON THE NURSERY SCHOOL STUDY

So far the Nursery School findings have been shown only as they
relate to those of the Infant School study. They are now listed below
in order of the frequency of entries under each category. It will be
noted under some of the groups that some categories appear which
have not been mentioned except in the Nursery School lists at the
end of each group reports since they are entirely different from those
of the Infant School study. In this table is given the total number of
incidents as observed during the sample periods of 300 minutes of
the participation of eighteen teachers.

Total no.
of contacts
from the 18
teachers

**N.1. "Contributes categorical information, provides
intellectual information and ideas, confirms and invites
confirmation of information from the child."**   1560

EXAMPLES.

Teacher: "We haven't got Susie today, have we?"
Child: "Good job she hasn't got Asian 'flu."
Teacher: "No, she hasn't got 'flu, she's going to have a new pair of shoes."

Teacher (to child building a canal): "We can't run the water right down the
canal, because of the grid."

Teacher: "Do you know what that colour is? It's called Prussian blue, that's
dark blue."

**N.2. "Invites spontaneous information and ideas from the
child."**   891

EXAMPLE

Child: "Miss X, come and look at my picture."
Teacher (looking at painting): "Oh, that's lovely, who is that?" (pointing to
figure)
Child: "My Mummy."
Teacher: "Your Mummy's very pretty."

N.3. "Clarifies a situation by explanation, explains the nature of materials, her own activities and the reasons for her questions, requests, refusals and actions." 828

EXAMPLES

"Jane, please keep your feet off the seat, people will get their clothes dirty from your muddy shoes."

A child was talking about her brother having a "side pencil".
Teacher: "A side pencil. Do you mean one with a clip on it to fix in his pocket?"

(Teacher refuses to put up a child's drawing) "Our walls are getting full—I will have to take some down to put more up."

N.4. "Spontaneously offers help, materials, permission information." 513

EXAMPLES

Teacher: "When you go to the Park, you may run as fast as you like."

Child: "Miss X, we are going to make a tunnel for this." (A red bus.)
Teacher: "Yes, that's right and you can take the big bricks."

N.5. "Stimulates the child's interest or draws the child's attention to something new. 276

EXAMPLES

Teacher: "Aren't these lovely pictures? Look, this is a car."

Child (showing a finished picture): "Look at this."
Teacher: "Oh, that is nice. Now would you like something fresh from the cupboard?"

Teacher: "Who wants to play football?"

E

N.6. "Corrects child's information, speech or manners."   157

EXAMPLES

Child interrupts teacher. "Sorry dear, wait until I've finished speaking."

Child (running over to the teacher holding a penny): "I got a sixpence."
Teacher: "Sixpence? No, not sixpence, a penny."

N.7. "Questions child to help him solve a problem."   146

EXAMPLES

Child puts a scarf on.
Teacher: "Do you need that on this morning? You think about it."

Teacher: "What is this colour?"
Child: "Orange."
Teacher: "And this one?" (child hesitates). "What colour is grass?"
Child: "Green."
Teacher: "Green, that's right."

N.8. "Questions or comments on the child's ideas, information or material."   89

EXAMPLE

Child (showing box): "Look! There's nothing inside!"
Teacher: "Nothing inside? Yes, there is."

Note on difference in the Infant School study between teachers of different ages of children

Nearly all the categories in this section show a rise in numbers after the children reach the age of six. Though no single category can on such small numbers be quoted alone as producing definite evidence, the consistency of this difference in so many categories is more suggestive of a marked indication that the conscious desire of children of the age of six and upwards for increased knowledge and skill has prompted the teachers to make more contacts of this kind. This tendency should also be considered in line with the greater number of contacts which the five-year-olds generally have of a protective and more socially personal nature. The teachers of the older children appear to need to spend less time on protecting, arbitrating and giving personal security to the children and are thus freed for more actual teaching. There is often a steeper rise between five and six than between six and seven. Indeed, in six categories (Nos. 1, 2, 5, 6, 8 and 9) six actually has a higher average than seven. In Nos. 3, 4 and 10, the seven-year-olds rank highest and only in Nos. 7 and 8 do the five-year-olds equal the seven-year-olds and in No. 10 the six-year-olds. In seven of the ten categories they fall below the averages for older children.

GROUP IB

Actions of the teacher where the material environment is used to assist in giving knowledge and experience

Two categories rank highest with 489 and 460 contacts. They are:

No. 13. "Helps by producing material."

This is done by every teacher to a considerable degree. No teacher of seven-year-olds falls below 11. This category is used rather more evenly throughout the sample than is the case in many of the preceding categories where teachers vary a good deal. In this category the majority range between 13 and 25, only four teachers scoring above 25. Production of the right material at the right time seems to be fully realised as important, but reliance on material is not overdone.

Child: "Can I have a strong box to make a house?"
Teacher: "Yes, dear." (She gets one.)

Child (a retarded and difficult child): "I want some string for a cloak."
Teacher: "Here it is." (She threads a large needle with wool and gives it to him.)

Teacher takes white tissue paper for a child who is making a fairy puppet. "Maybe you could do something with this."

No. 14. "The teacher herself attends to the care of material and equipment."

This shows considerable variation as between different teachers — six teachers have no recorded instances of it and possibly do more of it before or after the children are present in the classroom. Others spend considerable time on it. It was evident to the observers that careful attention had been paid to the care and arrangement of equipment and examples show that the teachers often help by fixing material in position for the children's use when it is too difficult for them to manage alone.

Teacher: "What we want is a small ledge for people to place their money on — you can sit inside and take the money."
(She gets cardboard and fixes it firmly with drawing pins)
Child: "Now I must put 'Paying Office' over the top."
Teacher: "Or you could call it 'Ticket Office'."
Child: "Oh, yes, that's a better name." He then writes and affixes his label.

(This example is cited more fully to show that the teacher's help produced active co-operation from the child. The teachers did not as a rule do things for the children in a way which rendered them passive or ineffective.)

Teacher: "Let me take that ragged lace off the bottom of the slip in case you fall over it." (Cuts it off a garment in which a child is about to dress up.)

Teacher: "I must mend that box." (Shows it to the child and mends it with cellotape while he watches.)

The next three categories with scores of 285, 254 and 252 are:

No. 15. "Helps by directing the use of material."

This type of help appears in the records of twenty-nine out of the thirty teachers. The average scores are 8 each for teachers of the two younger age-groups and 12 for teachers of seven-year-olds. The differences between individual teachers are less than in some of the other categories.

EXAMPLES

Teacher: "I think the dolls would look nicer with faces. I'll get some cotton wool and you can sew or paste it on and paint the face on it."

"It has to be stiff for scones. You have to roll it out. Use your hands to knead it together. . . . Now don't roll it too thin. You need it thick for scones."

"Now put the ruler at the bottom of your knitting and measure it up."

No. 16. "Helps by indicating the whereabouts of material."

This contact appears again in the records of all the teachers except one. Again as with No. 15, it is not among the categories which show greatest variation as between teachers. Averages are 9, 7 and 10 for teachers of five-, six- and seven-year-olds respectively.

EXAMPLES

Teacher: "There's a skirt in the dressing-up box if you look."

"There's some sugar in the green tin in my cupboard."

"See if you can find me a big screw in the nail box."

No. 17. "Helps by rendering assistance in the management of materials."

Averages are 7, 8 and 10 for teachers of five-, six- and seven-year-olds respectively and there is rather more variation between teachers.

EXAMPLES

Child: "I can't push the drawing pins in."
Teacher: "The wood's rather hard, dear — let me try." (This she does.)

Child finds it difficult to fix an elastic band on a newspaper doll. The teacher helps by holding the doll for her.

(Other similar instances of holding ruler while child marks off lengths to be cut off cardboard mast of toy ship while child secures it by making knot with string, etc.)

Teacher helps child to check accuracy of his calculation by sorting coins for him.

The last two categories Nos. 18 and 19 have total scores of 185 and 147.

No. 18. "Attends herself to the management of classroom materials."

This appears in the records of all except six of the teachers which may be significant since the teachers may have found time to do this work outside the free choice period. It is used most by the teachers of five-year-olds as would perhaps be expected since the older children would naturally be more independent, but differences are not large. Average scores are 8, 4 and 6 for the teachers of five-, six- and seven-year-olds respectively. Some arrangement by the teachers occurs in response to situations as they arise, as for example when it was time to feed the guinea pigs the teacher arranged chairs to ensure that the two children who were to feed them sat down to do it in a convenient place. Most good Infant School teachers, however, attend to arrangement of classrooms before the children arrive unless the children are ready to attend to this themselves, so the fact that scores in this category are not very high in no way indicates that the teachers were unaware of the importance of arranging the environment carefully.

Descriptions of the teachers make this point abundantly clear. Nearly all receive mention of showing care in this respect.

EXAMPLES

Teacher covers table with newspaper before painting begins.

Teacher puts out baking utensils. Fetches water for washing table and for filling the bath for water play.

Teacher puts the weighing table to rights and then removes finished paintings to make room for further activities.

No. 19. "Helps by suggesting the use of material."

All the teachers of seven-year-old children have scores, but three teachers in each of the other age groups are without scores. Averages are 4, 3 and 8.

EXAMPLES

Teacher: "Why not use the Wendy House as behind the stage, then when you come out, come through this door on to this (pointing) for the stage?"

"We could make a big class book and call it 'The Comic Circus' and write everything about the circus in it."

"If you take a tray of money you can find out for yourself."

"I should use crayons."

NURSERY SCHOOL STUDY

The only category which refers exclusively to the matter of material is:

N.9. "Reminds the child of the use and care of equipment."

There were few such contacts in the records, only six in all. However, the concern of the Nursery School teachers with providing suitable material and suggesting its appropriate use is evident in its inclusion in many of the broader groupings used in the Nursery School study. Moreover, many good Nursery School teachers spend much out-of-school time in making and repairing equipment and preparing the material environment before the children arrive and such instances of concern with material would not appear in the sampled periods.

EXAMPLE

Teacher: "Carry the chair properly. Not like that, dear, that's not the way to carry a chair."

General note on Group IB

In every category except No. 18, where the teacher herself is attending to arrangement of materials, the teachers of seven-year-old children came highest. Those of six-year-olds are no higher than those of five-year-olds and in some cases below them. The consistency of the seven-year-olds' rise perhaps suggests that at this age the children, and therefore their teachers, are more concerned with the finding of appropriate material and its most appropriate use, while at six as at five, the child's use of materials is more exploratory and less concerned with accurate and realistic representation so that the teachers are less engaged in seeking out and providing particular material for specific purposes and with directing or suggesting its use.

It is, however, evident that all these things are the concern of all the teachers and it is only a difference in proportion that differentiates the teachers of seven-year-olds from the others. The teachers are all actively concerned with the provision of adequate material and its care and use.

GROUP II

Actions of the teacher which particularly show concern with fostering and encouraging good social attitudes

Actions of rendering physical care, protection or comfort

No. 20. "Helps by attending to the child's clothing or physical comfort." 189

All teachers of the five-year-olds do this and half of them have thirteen or more instances of it in our sample of 180 minutes. One teacher only of six-year-olds has a high score of 28 and this teacher was working in a socially impoverished area. Except for this teacher and one other who has a score of 7, no teacher of children over six has a score of more than 5 and six teachers have no score at all. Averages are 12, 5 and 2 for teachers of five-, six- and seven-year-olds respectively. It seems evident from this and the two following categories that after the initial adjustment to school is over the children, having settled happily into a good Infant School, cease to need so much protection and comfort from their teachers. It is, however, still needed on occasions since the samples, even of the seven-year-olds, shows a total of 16 such contacts from the teachers concerned, while the teachers of six-year-olds show a total of 56, just under half those (117) of the teachers of five-year-olds. The Nursery School teachers appear to have still more of these contacts but since the contacts have been classified differently they are reported separately.

EXAMPLES

Teacher: "Are you well? You look pale. Have you got a cold? We'll go out to the toilet and see if you feel better."

Teacher supplies children with aprons and ties them on before they play with clay.

"Don't be afraid of dirtying your hands. You can wash them."

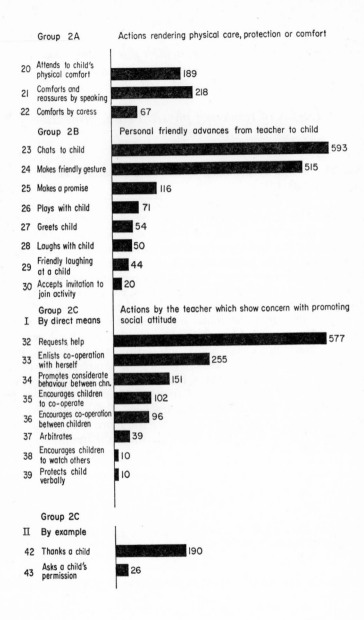

Group 2A   Actions rendering physical care, protection or comfort

20 Attends to child's physical comfort — 189

21 Comforts and reassures by speaking — 218

22 Comforts by caress — 67

Group 2B   Personal friendly advances from teacher to child

23 Chats to child — 593

24 Makes friendly gesture — 515

25 Makes a promise — 116

26 Plays with child — 71

27 Greets child — 54

28 Laughs with child — 50

29 Friendly laughing at a child — 44

30 Accepts invitation to join activity — 20

Group 2C
I   By direct means   Actions by the teacher which show concern with promoting social attitude

32 Requests help — 577

33 Enlists co-operation with herself — 255

34 Promotes considerate behaviour between chn. — 151

35 Encourages children to co-operate — 102

36 Encourages co-operation between children — 96

37 Arbitrates — 39

38 Encourages children to watch others — 10

39 Protects child verbally — 10

Group 2C
II By example

42 Thanks a child — 190

43 Asks a child's permission — 26

Reassures child who is afraid she has got paint on her cardigan.

"Wouldn't you like something to sit on?"

No. 21. "Comforts and reassures by speaking to a child." 218

This contact appears in the records of all except one teacher (of seven-year-old children). Again the average is higher for teachers of five-year-olds. Averages are 10, 7 and 5 for teachers of five-, six- and seven-year-olds respectively.

EXAMPLES

Teacher (to child who has tripped over in the garden): "Have you hurt yourself? Never mind—rub it—it only stings for a minute."

Child (in distress): "I've lost sixpence."
Teacher: "I shouldn't worry, dear, it will probably turn up when we clear up."

Child brings up clay puppet of a cat, one ear of which has broken off. "Its ear has come off."
Teacher: "Oh, pretend he has had a fight with another cat."

Child slips off her seat and looks startled.
Teacher: "Hello, I wondered where you were going."
(Child laughs.)

Child (worried about her model of a house): "The straw won't stick on."
Teacher: "Yes, dear, I know the straw does fall off — you must use better glue, not the paste."

No. 22. "Comforts or reassures by caress." 67

This appears in all except one of the records of teachers of five-year-olds. (The one who does not use it is the second highest in using verbal comfort with a score of 16.) Only half the teachers of six- and of seven-year-olds use it. Averages are 5, 1 and 1 for the three groups.

In the Nursery School study there is a contact listed under IIB, "Unspoken contacts", which comes very high indeed in the scores for Nursery School teachers but while undoubtedly most of these amount to a caress and many would relate to the giving of comfort, others would appropriately be described as friendly personal advances and seemed more appropriately classified with these. There seems, however, at least a strong suggestion that the comforting by caress is used more by teachers of the younger children, which is often more convincing than words to children of this age.

EXAMPLES

Child has wet himself.
Teacher puts her arm round him.
Teacher: "Cheer up, Peter, we'll soon have you dry and comfortable again."

Teacher goes up to a new child and takes her by the hand: "Hello, would you like to play with these children?"

Child is crying because another child will not let him have the toy tractor which he had allowed another child to use, but subsequently wanted it back again.
Teacher, having got the situation clear by questioning the children: "That was a good boy — you had a turn and then it was his turn, but you didn't give him many minutes to play with it did you?" (Putting her arm round the child. "Do you understand? We must take turns because we've only got one.")

Child: "Please may I have a drink?"
Teacher smiles and pats the girl's cheek.
"You're going to have your milk in a minute."

NURSERY SCHOOL STUDY

N.10. "Gives affection, comfort, personal attention or assurance."   519

EXAMPLES

Teacher (to child who has fallen down): "Oh, not very bad, Barry — don't worry."

Teacher takes child on her knee: "There! Is that better? Let's dry those tears."

N.11. "Warns the child of danger."   185

EXAMPLES

Teacher: "Careful, because we are near the road."

Teacher (to child on swing): "Debbie! Careful! Sit on properly."

Teacher: "Mind, Katie, mind, John! You might cut yourself on that spade."

N.12. "Suggests that the child ask help from his mother."   4

EXAMPLE

Teacher: "Look, what's that?" (Pointing to a hole in child's sock)
Child: "A hole."
Teacher: "You'll have to ask your Mummy to darn it."

Taken together, these three contacts overlap those of the Infant School study. Total scores show that the Nursery School teachers come not far below and probably therefore, higher than the teachers of five-year-olds who are in their turn much higher than teachers of older children.

Total scores of all three categories are:

Nursery School teachers	236 (proportional)
Teachers of five-year-olds	273
Teachers of six-year-olds	129
Teachers of seven-year-olds	69

It must also be remembered not only that (as mentioned already) a larger proportion of the Nursery School teachers' actions inevitably escape the recorders, but also that much of the physical care, protection and comfort of Nursery School children would be given by the "Nursery Helpers" whose records were not taken. Had the number of times the children in the Nursery Schools received such help been recorded they would almost certainly have been found to have received it from some adult considerably more frequently than the Infant School children did from their one and only teacher.

GROUP IIB

Personal friendly advances from teacher to child

Two categories, Nos. 23 and 24, come very high with totals of 593 and 515 contacts respectively. Both are used by every teacher.

No. 23. "Chats to a child."

Only four teachers have scores under 9. Averages are 17, 22 and 21. Nearly all the teachers use it a considerable amount and obviously do not regard it as a waste of time. Some of the examples were not fully audible to the observers and consisted of friendly talks with a child about his birthday cards or other treasures which were brought from home to show the teacher. Other examples relate to conversations with children about their holiday experiences and the teacher sometimes contributed her own experiences to the child's. A few short examples are:

Teacher (in passing, to a child who is reading): "Hello, old chap, have you got a good book?"
Child: "Yes, I like this one it's about Peter Pan and Captain Hook."
Teacher: "Yes, I love 'Peter Pan'."

Child: "This margarine has been in the 'fridge too long."
Teacher: "Have you got a 'fridge?"
Child: "Yes."
Teacher: "You are lucky."

Child: "Did you remember to bring my stuff?"
Teacher: "Yes, I did, Janet. The knot in my handkerchief helped me to remember."
Child: "Is the knot still in your handkerchief?"
Teacher: "Yes it is. Look, there it is!"

Teacher: "You are three feet, four inches tall — get some paper and I'll write it down (writing). Three feet four inches — your mother will be pleased."

Many of these informal conversations have educational value or pass on to something which results in expanding and enriching the child's ideas or knowledge, but they are classified here as the teacher's motive in starting the conversations was to make a friendly individual contact and show interest in the child rather than for a specific teaching purpose.

This contact does not appear as a single item in the Nursery School records though it is undoubtedly included in other categories.

No. 24. "Makes friendly gestures other than those needed for comfort."

This category bears a close relationship to No. 23 and again is used by all the teachers in varying amounts in all groups. Averages are 22, 12 and 17. It is possible that the teachers of the five-year-olds compensate for their lesser use of No. 23 by their greater use of No. 24 which fulfils a similar purpose. Some of the examples were simple instances of the teacher exchanging a sympathetic friendly smile with a child or nodding friendly approval or silently rendering a service which the child was requiring.

EXAMPLES

Child comes in for dinner money and seems hesitant.
Teacher holds her hand affectionately and says: "All right, Carol dear."

Boy (playing with toy telephone): "Will you talk to me?"
Teacher (smiles): "Yes, I will. Bring it to me please."

Girl: "It's my birthday."
Teacher kisses child: "We must light the candle for you later on and show the other children your cards and hear about your presents. What would you like to do as you are the birthday girl?"

The Nursery School study has such items included under several categories of which two especially come very close to it.

N.17 "Shows pleasure in the child's presence or interest in his personal condition."

and

N.18. "Unspoken friendly contacts."

Since, however, similar episodes are recorded elsewhere to cite merely those figures given here would suggest an underestimate of the amount which this type of contact is in fact made by the Nursery School teachers. There is inevitably very much overlap since Nursery School teachers are particularly inclined to combine friendly gestures with so much of their informal teaching.

The other categories in Group IIB fall very much in numbers below the first two.

No. 25. "Makes a promise to a child."

Has a score of 116 in all. It is, however, used by twenty-eight of the thirty teachers and averages are even between the age-groups — 4 in each case. It is classified here as it shows concern for the individual child and the intention to meet his wishes and further his purposes. It is not listed as such in the Nursery School categories, but is included in N.22, "Agrees to grant requests for objects, help or permission, after postponement". Its proportional score is very similar to those of the Infant School teachers and has also an average of 4 per teacher.

EXAMPLES OF NO. 25

"I'll look in my cupboard and see if I've got some (cardboard) money for you to use."

Child: "Can we show Miss M. this lovely Dutch picture book?"
Teacher: "She's not here today, but when she comes back you can."

"You really must stop now — you can go on again this afternoon."

Child: "Would you like to come and see my doll's house? I've made it bigger."
Teacher: "Yes, dear, in two minutes."

No. 26. "Plays with child by joining in spontaneously."

This scores a total of 71 episodes. Teachers of five- and six-year-olds have an average of 2 contacts and those of seven-year-olds 3, but it does not occur at all in the records of nearly half the teachers in each age-group. It is probable that the size of the classes makes it difficult for teachers to find time to do this very often.

In the Nursery School category N.15, "Shares child's feelings and imaginative play, laughter, talks and jokes," there is a considerably higher proportional score than that for teachers of five- and six-year-olds, but the wording is, of course, broader and admits certain incidents which do not entail "play". Nursery School teachers show an average of 5 contacts per teacher under N.15.

EXAMPLES OF No. 26 (Infant School Study)

Child with improvised ice cream box shouts "Ices, 3*d*. each!"
Teacher quickly puts out cardboard money.
Teacher (to another child): "Come on, we must buy an ice." She gives 6*d*. to the seller and says, "One, please, and I want some change."

Teacher shuffles the Lotto cards and plays with the children.

Teacher sits on the cart with the children.
"Shall I have a ride too?"

No. 27. "Greets a child."   (54 contacts in all)

This appears in the record of seven of the teachers of five-year-olds, six teachers of six-year-olds and only four of seven-year-olds — averages are 3, 2 and 1.

Nursery School teachers score higher than the teachers of an Infant School group (average 7) (see N.16). Moreover, they may well have certain additional items from the category N.17, "Shows pleasure in the child's presence", which in the Infant School study would have been included under Category No. 27. It is the younger children to whom personal greetings often mean most since the older ones are often more sure of their acceptance and welcome. Moreover, in schools established on active lines, the older children are often at work before the teacher arrives in the classroom so occasions for greeting the children individually are probably fewer.

F

EXAMPLES

Teacher (as child arrives at school): "How are you, Roger? Better?"

Teacher, having greeted several children individually, says to one: "Hello, Mary, I didn't expect to see you this morning. Are you quite better now?"

"Good morning, come along in."

No. 28. "Laughs with a child."

The total number of recorded episodes are 50 and it appears in the records of twenty out of the thirty teachers. Averages are 2, 1 and 3, the teachers of seven-year-olds using it most.

In the Nursery School study it is included in N.15, "Shares the child's . . . laughter . . . or jokes", but since it is combined with other sharing, the figures cannot be compared with the above.

EXAMPLES OF NO. 28

Child: "I have the bottom of my Mum's saucepan for a drum at home."
Teacher (laughing): "A good thing too! Do you use her wooden spoon too?"
(They both laugh.)

Teacher (to child making a puppet): "Shred the cotton wool a bit more to cover the head, it looks bald like that."
(Child and teacher laugh.)

Child laughs and says: "Miss — , don't tell us to pack up yet."
Teacher (laughs): "No, I won't."

Child: "Here's a sandwich for you — it's fifteen cents."
Teacher: "How much?"
Child: "Fifteen cents."
Teacher: "Robbery!"
(They both laugh.)

No. 29. "Friendly laughing at a child, but not in mockery."

(44 episodes)

This is only done by three teachers of the five-year-olds and four of six-year-olds, but seven of the teachers of seven-year-olds have scores. It is probably the seven-year-old classes which would contain more children capable of sufficient detachment to be able to enjoy a joke at their own expense. It is characteristic of these good teachers that no record exists of any laughing at the child in mockery or in a way which caused embarrassment to a child. Average scores are 1, 1 and 3. The category does not appear in the Nursery School study.

EXAMPLES OF NO. 29

Teacher to a child having difficulties beating a rhythm on a drum (taking his hands to help him): "Bounce, bounce, bounce! Come on, more jumpy movements." (She laughs.) "Ah, now you've got it."

Child brings a book of wallpapers into the room. The teacher takes it to a group of girls who are making a sweet shop. Having thanked the child she laughs and says, "It's like a miracle. It's just what we wanted."

Child in a group of children who are making a frieze of ducks: "I've cut the body out, now do I throw it away?"
Teacher (laughing): "Oh no!" (She demonstrates to the boy how to use the cutting.)

Occasionally the friendly laughter at the child is not done to the child but to the observer.

EXAMPLE

Teacher to observer: "Look, he is measuring in inches all the way across the playground." (Both laugh.)

No. 30. "Plays with child by accepting an invitation to join in an activity."

(20 episodes)

Only ten teachers have scores. The numbers are too small for averages to be meaningful.

It is possible that the children having adapted to the conditions of large classes with only one teacher do not make many requests of this kind since they see the teacher busily occupied.

EXAMPLES

Child playing in the Wendy House: "Have a cup of tea, Miss — ?"
The teacher sits down and takes the cup handed to her, pretending to drink. Then enters into conversation with the child.

Boy (wishing to play Lotto): "Come and play with me with Lotto."
Teacher: "Just a minute till I've got this arranged." (Settles a group of children by providing more clay and boards — then the child calls her again.)
Teacher: "I'm coming." Moves to the group playing Lotto, sits down and joins in the game.

Child brings potatoes to the teacher: "Here you are!"
Teacher: "Oh, thank you! How much are they?"
Child: "Two and six!"
Teacher: "I will pay for them. That's two and six. Is that right?"

In the Nursery School study this contact is included in N.15 "Shares the child's imaginative play". The number of instances in N.15 is much higher than in any age-group of the Infant School teachers but also includes other contacts.

No. 31. "Plays with child by asking to join in activity."

This occurs only twice in the whole of the records — two teachers have one contact each.

EXAMPLE

Teacher goes over to a group who are acting: "It looks rather exciting over here. I think I'll come and watch. May I?" (She helps to draw in other children as an audience to encourage the play.)

NURSERY SCHOOL STUDY

N.13. "Grants immediately the child's request for help, objects, attention or permission."   535

EXAMPLE

Child (holding up a nurse's apron): "Will you do this up for me?"
Teacher (ties apron): "Playing nurses are you?"

N.14. "Shows admiration for or interest in a child's clothes, possessions or productions or confidence in the child's relatives or interest in his home life."   533

EXAMPLES

Teacher: "Did you take your Daddy round the nursery?"

Teacher: "What a pretty jumper! Is it a new one?"

Child: "The Doctor is coming to see my Daddy."
Teacher: "Yes, poor Daddy! He's in bed with tonsilitis, Mummy told me."

N.15. "Shares child's feelings and imaginative play, laughter, talks or jokes."   361

EXAMPLES

Child pretends that it is after dinner.
Teacher: "Yes, I see, darling, so it is afternoon now."

"Tommy's come back hasn't he? That's nice for you isn't it? I am glad."

Teacher (being led away to prison): "I might try to escape."
Child: "You're all tied up, you can't get away."

N.16. "Greets or draws a child into a social situation."   20

EXAMPLE

"Good morning, Paul! Hello, Tom."

N.17. "Shows pleasure in child's presence or interest in his personal condition."   15€

EXAMPLES

Teacher: "John, show your sore finger to sister."

Child: "I wasn't well yesterday."
Teacher: "You weren't well, oh dear, but now you're better, eh! We haven't seen that nice face for such a long time."

N.18. "Unspoken friendly contacts."   7

EXAMPLE

Teacher sits down and takes child on her lap watching other children playing

---

As one would expect from good Nursery School teachers, the records abound in evidence of friendly personal interest in the children which is also reflected in the way in which many of the contacts which come into other categories are made.

GROUP IIC

*Actions of the teacher which show concern with
promoting social attitudes (i) by direct
means and (ii) by example*

No. 32. "Requests the child's help or co-operation."

This is by far the largest contact under this group. It shows a total of 577 contacts and is used by all the teachers nearly always to a considerable degree though there is some variation between teachers. Averages are 18, 19 and 21 for teachers of five-, six- and seven-year-olds respectively. This provides good evidence that far from the sometimes expressed belief that these methods mean leaving the child entirely to his own devices, good and experienced teachers have no hesitation in asking for, as well as giving, help and co-operation.

The Nursery School study also shows its highest number of contacts under N.19, "Asks or invites the child's help or co-operation". The average is 26 which is higher than any Infant School group.

EXAMPLES OF NO. 32

Teacher: "Please tidy the room up — after play, it's music time."

"Just help me carry your ship over there, will you?"

Teacher (to child whose wood has split): "It wants reinforcing — hand me the pincers, love. Thank you."

"Would you keep off this part of the floor, I would like to put paper down here."

"Bring me a chair, please."

"Go and ask if I can speak to John Williams, please."

No. 33. "Enlists co-operation between the child and herself."

This category comes very near to the above and also shows a high number of contacts, 255 in all. It appears in the records of all the teachers except one and the spread of variation between teachers is not as great as in many other categories. Averages are 8, 10 and 7 for teachers of five-, six- and seven-year-olds respectively. The Nursery School study does not separate it from N.19 though there is a category: "Demands the child's help or co-operation" (N.21), which scores an average of 6 per teacher.

EXAMPLES OF No. 33 (Infant School Study)

A marble has been lost. Teacher who has been attending to other matters says to a boy, "Oh, you're not looking for marbles."

Teacher: "How about playing a tune? Come on, we'll clap it together. . . . Now let's say it. . . . Now we'll try with out instruments."

Teacher: "Take a layer of this (paper), but don't press it down too much — then a layer of paste like this — you do some."

Boy: "Can I play in the shop?"
Teacher: "Yes, let's (both) pull the shop out."

Teacher: "Bring a ruler and we'll measure where the middle should be."

Teacher: "Tell me about it."

No. 34. "Promotes social attitudes between children or considerate behaviour."   151

This contact appears in the records of 24 of the thirty teachers. Average scores are: 6, 5 and 4 for teachers of five-, six- and seven-year-olds respectively.

In the Nursery School study this type of action by the teacher is described in detail (see N.20). The proportional number of such contacts is very considerably higher than that of any of the Infant School groups. They show an average of 23 contacts per teacher. It is possible that the older children need rather less help of this kind having become more social. It is certainly evident that Nursery School teachers give a great deal of such help. It would be interesting had it been possible to know whether more help went to the children under four years of age.

EXAMPLES OF No. 34 (Infant School Study)

Teacher: "Haven't you got enough hammers?"
Boy: "No, we've only got three."
Teacher (producing a fourth hammer from cupboard): "You must share them. When you've finished hammering for a while, put it down and then someone else can use it and don't take the hammers belonging to Mrs. E.'s children."

"We are very crowded this afternoon, having everyone inside, so when you set to work, just watch where you are going."

Teacher: "How long have you had this drum, old chap? A long time? Let someone else have a turn."

A boy is crying.
Teacher: "What's wrong?"
Boy: "He pushed me off the table."
Teacher: "Who did?"
The boy who did it points to himself.
Teacher: "What was that for?"
Boy: "I asked him to get off the table and he wouldn't."
Teacher: "You've hurt him, haven't you?"
Boy nods.
Teacher: "Well, you'd better take him away and make him happy again." (Pats head of the boy who was crying and says, "You get off another time when you are asked.")

Teacher: "Well, ask him nicely to leave your boat alone."

No. 35. "Directs or encourages the children to co-operate." 102

This category comes very close to the above and again shows slightly more records from the teachers of five-year-olds. Twenty-seven teachers all have scores ranging from 1 to 10. Averages are 4, 3 and 3. This contact is, of course, included in the very comprehensive N.20 of the Nursery School study.

EXAMPLES OF No. 35 (Infant School Study)

Teacher (after watching children's efforts at the music table speaks to one boy who is beating out a rhythm successfully): "You are good, you be the teacher and teach the others."

Teacher: "Children, if anyone is interested, we could do with a lot more houses and shops and a block of flats."

Teacher: "Oh, you must listen to the Ringmaster, he's there to help you. Don't have more than two or three on the stage at the same time."

No. 36. "Enlists co-operation between children."　　96

Again this bears a close relationship to the two categories above Nos. 34 and 35. Twenty-seven teachers have scores. Averages are 4, 2 and 4.

The Nursery School study includes "promoting co-operation" in category N.20. Since the Infant School contacts Nos. 34, 35 and 36 are all included in the Nursery Schools N.20, it would seem appropriate to add the Infant School averages to bring them into relation with the Nursery School teachers' very high average. Even so, the Nursery School teachers still outnumber them, having an average of 23 as against the averages of 14, 10 and 11 for the teachers of five-, six- and seven-year-olds respectively.

EXAMPLES OF No. 36 (Infant School Study)

Child: "I want some tape for my apron."
Teacher: "Ask Pamela about tape for your apron. She's got some."

Teacher: "Is that how much (string) you want?"
Boy: "No, I need more than that"
Teacher: "Go with him Charles and measure again."

Teacher: "Here's some blue paper to make the sky. Who'd like to help David to make the picture?"

No. 37. "Arbitrates." (39 contacts

Only four of the teachers of seven-year-olds have records and only one of these has two, giving an average of only $\frac{1}{2}$. The teachers of the other two age-groups both have an average of 2 and seven teachers in both groups have scores.

Nursery School teachers also have scores for the same contact (N.24) and have an average of 4. This result raises the question as to whether the older children being more accustomed to co-operating with other children present fewer occasions when the teacher needs to intervene to settle quarrels or disputes.

EXAMPLES OF NO. 37 (Infant School Study)

An argument arises between two girls playing in a draper's shop.
Teacher (to one of the girls): "Tell her how much tape you need." (To the other girl): "And then you tell her how much it is."

Teacher (to a boy who is teasing another): "John, help Ernie and leave Chris alone."

A dispute arises in the post office. Teacher turns and one boy says, "If I give him 1/- and it costs me 5*d*., I shall have 8*d*. change, shouldn't I?" Teacher shakes her head: "No. Look, find the box of money."
She helps the child to count twelve pennies and then takes five away, counting aloud, and carefully. "Now see how much."

Teacher: "Anthony, go away, please. Stephen was there first." (Checks with the other children that Stephen was there first to which they agree.)

Teacher intervenes in a dispute over a game of draughts: "Wait a minute! Where were you playing?"
(She is shown.)
"Oh well, you've lost it I'm afraid, that's the game."

No. 38. "Provides an audience by suggesting that other children shall watch." 10

Only five teachers have records of using this contact. Two are teachers of five-year-olds and three of six-year-olds. It does not appear in the Nursery School records.

EXAMPLE OF NO. 38

Teacher: "Children, if there is anybody free, perhaps you'd like to come and watch this play." (Later) "I've enjoyed that — I'm afraid I must go away now as there are one or two children wanting me, but you children would like to stay and see the rest, wouldn't you?"

No. 39. "Takes verbal action to protect a child."   10

Only six teachers have a record, four of whom are teachers of five-year-olds. In the Nursery School study it would probably be included in N.20, "Reminds the child that others have feelings", and in Section IIA (N.11), "Warns the child of danger". It would, perhaps, be more appropriate to have classified this contact with IIA since some of the examples are of warning the child about danger to himself, e.g. to a child using a saw the teacher said: "Mind your finger, old chap." Others, however, relate to intervening to prevent one child hurting or upsetting another, for example, by thrusting him out of the group.

No. 40. "Takes physical action to protect a child."

The only recorded incident was when a teacher caught the arm of an angry child to prevent a blow to another child. It seems, therefore, appropriate to place these categories here though some of the incidents recorded under 32 do not relate to developing social attitudes so much as to impressing the need for caution in the interests of the child's own safety.

No. 41. "Rejects an offer of help."

This category has been placed last since it seems a negative way of promoting social behaviour. There is only one record of it from each of five teachers of children over six. Some of the incidents are unfortunate, reflecting the very rare instances when even these good teachers misunderstand a child who is wanting to help by saying "I haven't time to attend to you now", but others give an explanation which certainly raises the apparent rejection to the level of helping the child to see another's point of view as, for example, when a child offered to fetch something for the teacher from the Headmistress and she said "Well, not today — the Secretary is away and Miss X is far too busy", or when a child wanted to do something for another child and the teacher explained that the other child wished to do it himself.

In the Nursery School study, too, there were rare instances of the teacher rejecting a child's offer of help, but very courteously, and with an explanation why it is not wanted at the time (see N.25). The average here is only 1 per teacher which is low considering the inexperience of very young children which is liable to lead them to offer inappropriate help.

IIC (ii)

The following two categories both illustrate how the teacher influences the child to acquire good social attitudes by her own example of courtesy. Both also occur in the Nursery School study.

No. 42. "Thanks a child."   (190 incidents recorded)

Only two teachers are without scores. Averages are 7, 8 and 13.

Nursery School teachers have an average of 5 but would have more contacts than are shown in N.23, "Thanks a child for help or gift", as some also occur in N.26, "Accepts child's help or gifts", which, as is illustrated in the example given, is often accompanied by thanks.

EXAMPLES OF NO. 42

Many examples are of a simple "Thank you" when the child offers a sweet, finds objects which had been mislaid, etc. Sometimes the thanks are expanded somewhat, for example:

Teacher: "Thank you very much, boys. It was very kind of you to bring the toad for us to see."

"Thank you very much, Stephen (to a child clearing table). You are a good boy."

No. 43. "Asks a child's permission."   26

This appears in the records of about half the teachers in each age-group and the average is one throughout. The Nursery School study has only one incident in the total records.

EXAMPLES

Teacher (leaning over a child to reach some paper): "Excuse me, Edward, please."

Teacher: "May I borrow a pair of scissors, please?"

NURSERY SCHOOL STUDY

N.19. "Asks or invites child's help or co-operation, or draws attention to the child's ability to help himself."   773

EXAMPLES

"Nigel, try to keep the clay on the table, please."

"Would you like to throw that envelope away for me?"

N.20. "Contacts likely to promote a good social attitude or an increase in social awareness by any of the following means:

By recognising or promoting co-operation.

By suggesting that one child offers or gives, asks or accepts help from another.

By suggesting that one child invites another to play with him.

By pointing out the discomfort of one child to another.

By reminding children that others have feelings."   695

EXAMPLES

Teacher: "Don't sit on his legs, darling, I'm sure you'll hurt him."

Child: "Bobby won't let me go upstairs."
Teacher: "Perhaps you haven't asked him nicely. It's very important how you ask. Go and ask Bobby nicely."

Teacher: "Stephen, this is rather too heavy to carry on your own, help him, John."

Children say they don't want Tommy.
Teacher: "Why not? I'm sure he will be very helpful to your play."

N.21. "Demands a child's help or co-operation."   178

EXAMPLE

"Ronnie, go and hang up your coat."

N.22. "Agrees to grant requests for objects, help or permission after postponement."   149

EXAMPLE

Child (doing a puzzle): "Will you help me?"
Teacher: "Yes, in a minute."

It is perhaps not self-evident why this contact should be placed in this group but it is certainly one of the ways in which young children learn that the teacher has to be shared because of the needs of other children and becomes aware that he can share without losing her interest and help which enables him to accept the idea of sharing.

N.23. "Thanks a child for help or gift."   145

This is generally expressed simply as "Thank you, Sam, thank you, Joe", etc.

EXAMPLE

Teacher (taking a sweet): "Oh lovely, thank you!"

N.24. "Arbitrates in a dispute."   123

EXAMPLES

Teacher: "Mary, you've had the pram a long time. Will you let Linda have a turn?"

Teacher (as twins squeal): "Kathleen, Kathleen! They belong to Margaret, you are a pair aren't you?"

N.25. "Refuses child's help, gift or production."   39

EXAMPLE

Child comes to the teacher with a jar of water
Teacher: "Did you think I wanted it? We've nothing to put in it."

Again perhaps an explanation is needed. This contact at first sight appears to be a discouragement rather than a promotion of social attitudes, but when the child's intention to help is recognised as in the above example he does not feel rebuffed, but is often assisted in learning how to help appropriately.

N.26. "Accepts the child's help or gifts."   37

EXAMPLE

Child: "It's for you." (Showing picture he has painted.)
Teacher: "For me? Oh, but don't you want it for Mummy?"
Child: "No, you can take it home."
Teacher: "Oh, thank you! Would you like to tell me about your picture?"

N.27. "Apologises to child." 34

This contact (as also N.23) would be classified as IIC (ii) since it is concerned with promoting good social attitudes by example. It is given here simply in order to preserve the sequence in the contacts from the Nursery School study in Group IIC in numerical order of frequency.

EXAMPLE

Teacher (knocking against child's house): "Sorry, Bill, I trod on the back."

N.28. "Ask child's permission." (1 contact only in the records)

This too is a IIC (ii) contact.

EXAMPLE

Teacher (to child who has just finished a drawing): "May I see your book?"

General note on Section II

The chief features that emerge from this section is abundant evidence of the warmth and friendliness of the teachers and of their unhesitating readiness to give children full opportunity and encouragement to show in their turn friendly and helpful behaviour towards the teacher and to each other. With regard to differences in teachers of different age groups, it is clear that in Group IIA the teachers of younger children have considerably more of these contacts than do the teachers of the older age groups. This is to be expected in view of the need of young children, making their first entry to school, for personal care, protection and comfort. Group IIB (Personal friendly advances) from teacher to child does not show this difference since the teachers of seven-year-olds have as many records as those of the five-year-olds. Group IIC (Direct attempts to promote social attitudes in the children) shows a tendency for teachers of younger Infant School children to use it more than those of seven-year-olds, while Nursery School teachers use it most.

G

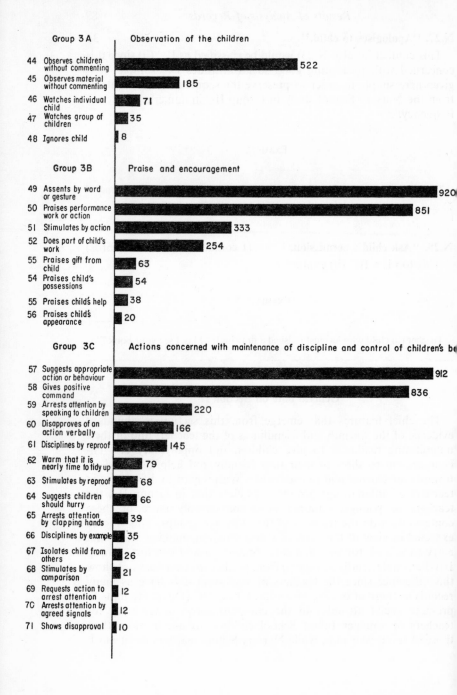

Group 3A   Observation of the children

44	Observes children without commenting	522
45	Observes material without commenting	185
46	Watches individual child	71
47	Watches group of children	35
48	Ignores child	8

Group 3B   Praise and encouragement

49	Assents by word or gesture	920
50	Praises performance work or action	851
51	Stimulates by action	333
52	Does part of child's work	254
53	Praises gift from child	63
54	Praises child's possessions	54
55	Praises child's help	38
56	Praises child's appearance	20

Group 3C   Actions concerned with maintenance of discipline and control of children's be

57	Suggests appropriate action or behaviour	912
58	Gives positive command	836
59	Arrests attention by speaking to children	220
60	Disapproves of an action verbally	166
61	Disciplines by reproof	145
62	Warn that it is nearly time to tidy up	79
63	Stimulates by reproof	68
64	Suggests children should hurry	66
65	Arrests attention by clapping hands	39
66	Disciplines by example	35
67	Isolates child from others	26
68	Stimulates by comparison	21
69	Requests action to arrest attention	12
70	Arrests attention by agreed signals	12
71	Shows disapproval	10

GROUP III

Ways in which the teacher establishes a setting which is favourable to education and which are of equal importance to the child's emotional, social and intellectual welfare

IIIA

Observation of the children

The characteristic of this group is that the categories are concerned with watching without commenting. Undoubtedly in all the participation of teachers, observation precedes comment but here are recorded the times which the teacher is prepared to spend in merely watching. It has not been recorded in the Nursery School study.

No. 44. "Observes children without commenting." 522

This is done by all except one of the teachers and shows considerable variation. The tendency of teachers of six-year-olds is to use this contact less, which brought forth a comment from one of the observers, who also studied the records of many of the other observers, that the teachers of five-year-olds who used it so much were apparently watching newcomers with the purpose of understanding their needs, while the teachers of seven-year-olds appeared to be storing up their observations to raise questions or make comments later in "Discussion periods" — whereas the teachers of six-year-olds tended to comment at the time, possibly because they did not expect the child's capacity to wait, for the solution of problems would be so high and their need for immediate stimulus and encouragement would be greater. Averages are 18, 13 and 22. The teachers of seven-year-olds undoubtedly find silent observation worth while. No teacher of this age group has a record of less than 7.

EXAMPLES OF NO. 44

Children are working on a model.
Boy: "Do we put clay on now?"
Teacher: "Not yet."
She returns to one boy and watches him for a few minutes. Then goes to the children working with waste material — watches for a while.

Teacher hears a glass fall and looks up. She sees that it is being picked up and says nothing.

Teacher watches boy trying to find a painting with a clean back on which he can paint another picture. (To the observer.) "He isn't satisfied with any of those. I wonder what he will do now. I suppose I really ought to give him a piece."

Teacher continues to sort the art pictures, watching the group painting at the same time.

No. 45. "Observes material or child's work without commenting."
185

Here again, the teachers of seven-year-olds use it most. There is no teacher in this group who has no score. Seven teachers have no score at all. Again the teachers of six-year-olds fall below the other two groups, possibly for the reasons suggested above. Averages are 5, 3 and 11. This category shows much less variation between teachers than does No. 44 and is less used. The total number of contacts is only 185 as compared with 522 for No. 44. The child himself is evidently the main object of the teachers' observation.

EXAMPLES OF NO. 45

Teacher crosses to table where children are writing stories. Looks at their work, but does not comment.

Teacher moves to table where child is making a picture for a toy cinema. Stands and observes for a moment. Then gives some advice to the child.

Teacher (to observer): "There are some beautiful houses over there" (points them out).

No. 46. "Provides audience by watching an individual child."   71

Here the object is not only to observe the child but to give him the satisfaction of being observed. As one might expect, teachers of five-year-olds do this rather more since the young child is often the most eager for a grown-up admirer of his exploits. Averages are 4, 1 and 2, the six-year-olds again falling below the other groups.

EXAMPLES OF NO. 46

Boy helps the teacher to add up the dinner money, methodically making up the shillings without any help, while teacher watches.
Teacher: "That's right, 5/6d."

Girl brings her story book.
Teacher: "Oh, what a long one! Read it to me, Janice."
Girl reads while teacher listens.
Teacher: "That's a lovely story, Janice. Your book is going to be a very nice one."

Girl, making a fan, is in difficulties. Teacher demonstrates and then says, "You see if you can finish it." She sits and watches the child who successfully manipulates the paper.
Teacher: "Bravo!"

No. 47. "Provides audience by watching a group of children."   35
This is done by sixteen teachers. Averages are one in each group.

EXAMPLES OF NO. 47

Teacher goes to the acting corner. Sits on a chair to watch. She is very interested, remains three minutes.

Puppet show about to begin. Child says: "Come on Miss Y, come and listen."
Teacher assents and she and the observer form part of the audience.

Child: "Can you see what we are doing?"
Teacher: "Yes, I'm watching you."

Teacher goes to a corner where a child is reading to others. Looks over the child's shoulder as she reads and helps her when she hesitates over a word.

No. 48. "Ignores child because not noticed."   8

This is, of course, a direct negative of the above categories and of the IIIA contact and is chiefly remarkable for its very low score when we consider the size of classes and the many claims on the teacher's attention. Only five teachers have any record. It is perhaps worth noting here that in all the records there is only one instance of deliberately ignoring a child.

EXAMPLE OF NO. 48

Girl working on a sweet shop says: "Miss X, we've got it nice."
Teacher does not hear as she is crossing the room to attend to another child.

IIIB

Praise and encouragement

The first two categories have very high scores.

No. 49 has a total of 920 contacts and No. 50 of 851. These contacts are "Assents by word or gesture" and "Praises child's performance, work or action". These two contacts and No. 51 which comes next with 333 contacts "Stimulates by encouragement" are all mainly concerned with supporting the child's achievement or ideas which at the Infant School age is often the way in which the child appreciates his acceptability as a person since he himself is beginning to be very much identified with his desire for knowledge and skill and is anxious for reassurance about his ability to win these. The next most numerous category, No. 52 (254 contacts), is also concerned with encouraging the child by helping him with his work and of the more personal matters which are praised by the teacher the totals are smaller, ranging from the lowest (20 contacts) No. 56, "Praises the child's appearance", to No. 53 (63 contacts), "Praises the child's gift". Though smaller, however, these contacts show that the teacher is aware that children of this age have by no means outgrown the need for praise and encouragement on more personal matters.

No. 49. "Assents by word or gesture."

This contact is used by every teacher to a considerable degree. There is less variation between teachers in this category than in many others. Averages are 23, 33 and 37 for teachers of five-, six- and seven-year-olds respectively. The lower number for five-year-olds (though it is by no means low) may be because many five-year-olds are in less doubt about their ability to achieve what they are aiming at being still prepared to accept symbolic representatives of objects in the real world rather than to criticise their own products by standards of reality. They may, therefore, possibly need rather less "assent" from the adult.

The Nursery School study has a category N.29 "Accepts the child's information and ideas", which clearly comes close to No. 49. Here the Nursery School teachers come slightly above those of five-year-olds, a proportional total of 239 contacts as compared with the five-year-olds' 225 which gives the Nursery School teachers an average of 24 which may, of course, actually be higher. It must, however, be borne in mind that in the Nursery School, children arrive at school often in a leisurely manner and get easy access to the adult. This means that they have many opportunities of offering information to the teacher about home interests and these would be included under category N.29 which is a somewhat broader heading than the Infant School's "Assents by word or gesture" which implies an agreement with a question in the child's mind or the granting of requests, as are illustrated in the examples selected. There were other examples where the teacher merely nodded her agreement.

On this aspect the Nursery School study has, as already reported, two other categories N.13, "Grants immediately child's request for help, objects, attention or permission", and N.22, "where the granting of the requests is postponed." N.13 especially would undoubtedly contain some episodes which would be similar to those listed in the Infant School study under No. 49. The average of this category is 18, so this may compensate to some extent for the possible over-estimation of the "assents" factor in N.29. Category N.22 has an average of only 3 and is, in any case, less likely to overlap episodes recorded under No. 49.

EXAMPLES OF NO. 49 (Infant School Study)

Child: "Can I have a piece of drawing paper, please?"
Teacher: "Yes, dear, what are you making?"
Child: "I want to make a mask."
Teacher: "Yes, dear, I should think this size will do."

Child: "Can I have the pincers?"
Teacher (laughs): "Oh yes, I knew you wanted something."

Child (has written a letter): "Miss — , I want a stamp and the post office is closed."
Teacher: "Oh, so it is." Take a stamp and gives it to the child.

No. 50. "Praises child's performance, work or action."   851

Again this contact is used by every teacher. Averages are 29, 27 and 29. The high numbers give evidence of how generous these good teachers are in the matter of praise and encouragement. It will be evident later how much more frequently they use this stimulus rather than blame or reproof.

In the Nursery School study there is a category, N.32, "Commends the child's behaviour", which shows a proportional average of only 4 contacts per teacher, but since the Infant Schools' category here is wider and includes work and performance, this must be seen in relation to N.30, "Encourages child by admiration or approval of an achievement or production". This shows a proportional average of 11 contacts per teacher but even when added to N.32 falls very much below the Infant teachers since it gives an average of only 15. However, it may well be considerably higher in reality as not only might teachers have used it when not in the presence of the observer, but the Nursery Helpers would doubtless have used it, too.

EXAMPLES OF No. 50 (Infant School Study)

Child shows teacher a pattern.
Teacher: "Oh, I like that." (She smiles approvingly, pats him, saying, "Isn't it a good pattern?")

Child brings her book to show teacher.
Teacher: "That's a lovely book! Would you like a big one now? You deserve it."

Teacher looks at child's clay model and says: "That looks just like a Pekinese."
Child: "It is!"
Teacher: "Its very nice, dear, just like one."

No. 51. "Stimulates by encouragement." 333

Two teachers of five-year-olds have no record but it is a teacher of five-year-olds who has the highest record of 41 contacts. The other teachers all have records and show less striking variations. Averages are 10, 13 and 11 for the three age-groups.

The Nursery School study has three categories which overlap No. 51:

N.30 as mentioned above with an average of 11 contacts;
N.31 "Encourages by suggestion" (Average 9);
and N.33 "Encourages by reassurance" (Average 4).

Taken together these three would outnumber the records of any group of Infant teachers but N.30 would include episodes where finished achievements were praised which is not quite the same as stimulating to further achievement by encouragement.

EXAMPLES OF No. 51 (Infant School Study)

Girl who has been stitching, hands teacher her sewing.
Teacher: "You have cut out the corners. When you've stitched these down it will be finished. It will be lovely for the library corner."

Child: "Stephen's spoilt the model I made."
Teacher: "Oh, what a shame! They've spoilt your lovely church."
Child: "Stephen did it."
Teacher: "Well you could make another one on your own with another box, couldn't you?"

Child: "I'm going to make a seat. Will you come and help me?"
Teacher: "Well, have you any ideas yourself? Let me see how you thought of making it?" (Watches the child.)
"Yes, I thought of something like that too."
Child: "But it won't stand up properly."
Teacher: "Perhaps match sticks will help. I brought some this morning." (Supplies them.)

No. 52. "Helps by doing part of the child's work for him." 254

This is done mainly to encourage the child who has lost heart through some difficulty and the result of the teacher's help is almost always that the child takes up the work and goes on by himself. Only two teachers have no record. Teachers of five-year-olds tended to do less of this kind of helping — their average is 5 compared to 10 in both the other groups.

The Nursery School study has no record of this kind of help which possibly confirms the suggestion that since the younger children are less concerned with a realistic result they do not need this kind of help as much as do older children who are more aware of failure to achieve their goal in "work". Teachers of seven-year-olds fluctuate more than those of the other groups in the amount they use this contact. Some teachers use it much more than others who perhaps prefer other means of helping. Teachers of six-year-olds use it very consistently — it is possible that this may reflect the unwillingness of six-year-olds to wait as patiently for success as some seven-year-olds can do.

EXAMPLES OF NO. 52

Boy wishes to make cloak. Teacher threads a large needle with wool and gives it to him. He threads this through the top of the cloak and brings it to the teacher to fasten off.
Teacher: "Now you've done what you wanted."

Children making a model village. Teacher looks at the painted towelling (for the park), folds it in half and places it on the table model to see if it fits. She then marks the measurement and says to the child: "Now cut along this line."

Boy doing woodwork (discouraged).
Teacher: "I expect it is difficult. It is so thick. I'll come and see what I can do."
Teacher goes to the woodwork bench.
Teacher: "If I can just get it started I think it will be all right."

No. 53. "Praises child's gift."   63

This occurs in the records of seventeen teachers. Averages are 5 for teachers of five-year-olds and one for the other two groups.

The Nursery School study has N.26, "Accepts the child's help or gifts", which is not quite the same, though there would be some overlap. Proportional average is one.

EXAMPLES OF NO. 53

Child offers the teacher a card.
Teacher: "Isn't that nice, Susan? You've made an Easter card for me. I can have this one can I? Oh, a lovely stamp!"

Teacher: "Now what a lot of things you've brought this morning." A girl hands teacher several packets of seeds.
Teacher: "Oh, these are for the Nature Table are they? Lovely!"
Girl: "I've cut these pictures out for the Nature Book."
Teacher: "What beautiful little chicks! They are sweet!"

Teacher: "Oh, what lovely flowers Sandra. Thank you very much! Did Daddy grow them in his garden?"

Boy: "Miss —, here's a letter."
Teacher turns, smiles and takes it. "Is it to me?" . . . (reads it). Smiles at child and says: "That's a lovely letter. Thank you."

No. 54. "Praises child's possessions." 54

This occurs in the records of seventeen teachers. Averages are 1, 2 and 2.

This category does not appear in the Nursery School study.

EXAMPLES OF NO. 54

Child shows teacher some dolls' house furniture.
Teacher: "Oh, how lovely! Who made these?"
Child: "A man who lives with us cut them out."
Teacher: "They're jolly clever, aren't they?"

Child: "Look Mrs. G.!" (indicates necklace)
Teacher: "Isn't that lovely?"

Boy: "Look, I've got new shoes!"
Teacher: "They are nice."
Boy: "I've brought a box."
Teacher: "That's fine."
Child: "Here's a book about 'The Three Bears'."
Teacher: "How nice, that will help us with our play."

No. 55. "Praises child's help."   38

This appears in the records of thirteen teachers. Averages are almost equal, 1 in each group.

In the Nursery School study N.26, "Accepts the child's help or gift", has already been mentioned in relation to No. 53 and also has an average of 1 contact per teacher.

EXAMPLES OF NO. 55

Teacher (to child helping to clear the room): "That's right, Thea, the table goes over there."

Teacher (to child who has contributed to the class "News Book"): "That's a lovely story, Pam! I'll put a star on it. All the spellings are correct."

A boy finds a marble that was missing.
Teacher: "Oh, you've found one! Good!"
Girl: "Here are two more!"
Teacher: "Two, good!"

No. 56. "Praises child's appearance."   (20 contacts)

This is done by four teachers of five-year-olds. Only two teachers have records in the other two groups.

It does not occur in the Nursery School study as a separate category though it is sometimes involved in other categories such as "Shows pleasure in the child's presence".

EXAMPLES OF NO. 56

Girl: "Look at me!"
Teacher: "You do look smart."

NURSERY SCHOOL STUDY

The items listed here are those which are classified only under IIIB, not those already listed under other groups, even though they have some overlap with IIIB as has been shown above.

Total no.
of contacts
among 18
teachers

N.29. "Accepts a child's information and ideas.   717

EXAMPLE

Child: "We have built a bridge all this morning."
Teacher: "That's a good idea."

N.30. "Encourages the child by admiration or approval of an achievement or production."   334

EXAMPLES

Child shows stencils. "These two are beautiful. Try some more."

Child (doing up his coat): "Look!"
Teacher: "You can do it up. That's a good boy."

Teacher: "Yes, its coming on nicely."

N.31. "Encourages child by suggestion."   281

EXAMPLES

Teacher: "Are you going to put these flowers in water, John?"

Child (showing picture): "Look!"
Teacher: "You could stick it in something if you like."

N.32. "Commends child's behaviour."   132

EXAMPLE

Child: "Can I give a sweet to little Joyce?"
Teacher: "That is nice of you."

N.33. "Encourages by reassurance."   110

EXAMPLES

Alice: "I can't cut these wings for my bird properly."
Phyllis: "Neither can I."
Teacher: "When I show you, you can. I'm just coming."

Teacher: "That's better now."

GROUP IIIC

Actions of the Teacher which are concerned with maintaining discipline and control of the children's behaviour

These contacts fall into five main groups:
   (a) (Much the largest group) is concerned with giving positive directions, advice and suggestion to the children.
   (b) Stimulating effort or good behaviour.
   (c) Arresting attention.
   (d) Reproof.
   (e) Punishment.
(d) and (e) are the more negative approaches and (e) is very much smaller in number of incidents.
   The largest categories are Nos. 57 (912 contacts) and 58 (836) and are concerned with suggesting, advising and giving positive

commands. There is then a considerable drop to No. 59 (220 contacts) which is the first and probably the most intelligent of the methods of arresting attention, i.e. by speaking to the children. After that there is another considerable drop to two of the "Reproof" categories Nos. 60 (166 contacts) and 61 (145).

No. 62 (with 79 contacts) is more concerned with arresting attention and Nos. 63 and 64 with stimulating effort and good behaviour, as is also true of the next two categories Nos. 65 and 66. The numbers in these categories range from 68 to 35 contacts. No. 67 with a total of 26 contacts is the highest of the "punishment" categories, "Disciplines by isolation". No. 68 (with 21 contacts) is of the "Stimulation" character after which the numbers become very small. Nos. 69 and 70 (12 contacts in each) are concerned with arresting attention, as is also No. 74 with only 2 contacts. The other very small categories are concerned with reproof or punishment. This section very much confirms the statement which has been made that the better the teacher the less will punishment be needed. These good teachers resort to it very seldom. It is evident also on examination of the records that the so-called "Reproofs" are often very courteous and gentle.

No. 57. "Suggests or advises appropriate actions or behaviour." 912

Many of the suggestions and advice relate to how to achieve success in work and should perhaps have been included with IA for that reason. However, others are more concerned with behaviour and all are instances of the teacher exercising definite leadership which plays its part in giving the child a sense of security and purpose which is very relevant to the question of discipline so it seems appropriate to place it here. It is much used by all the teachers. Only four of the eighteen teachers have records below 17 incidents and these four have 11 and upwards. Averages are 26 for teachers of five-year-olds, and 32 and 33 for teachers of six- and seven-year-olds respectively.

The Nursery School study has a category N.40, "Advises, reminds or suggests an acceptable form of behaviour", but it has a very small record (only 5 contacts from the eighteen teachers) and it is probable that this kind of help was implicit in contacts which have been classified under other headings and were not separated out very much when the analysis was made, possibly because the approaches of suggesting and advising were made in a very subtle and informal way. The Nursery School study shows many more instances of specific commands which are more self-evident but on examining the records of the Nursery School teachers I should very much doubt whether, in fact, they used commands more than suggestions.

EXAMPLES OF No. 57 (Infant School Study)

Teacher: "You could make a house for the Doctor because we do need one."

Teacher: "I think before we cut them out we ought to do the painting."
Child: "There's no room to paint."
Teacher: "We shall have to clear one of the tables."

Teacher: "I should wash your hands, Tommy."

Child: "They won't lend me the basket."
Teacher: "I should ask them nicely and I'm sure they will."

Teacher (to child who says he does not know what to put in his drawing): "You have a little think."

Teacher (to new child): "Would you like to come and play with these children?"

Girl brings teacher a cup of tea.
Teacher: "I'd like to have it with a saucer, please."

No. 58. "Gives a positive command."   836

Again this is done by all the teachers but less with those of the five-year-old children. Only two teachers of five-year-olds have scores of more than 14, whereas only three of the other twenty teachers fall below 15. There is more variation between the amount used by different teachers than in No. 57.

The Nursery School category N.35, "Gives a child a specific order", shows an average of 13 which is the same as (and, therefore, probably higher than) teachers of five-year-olds.

"Oh, Victor, get the map!"

To class: "Will you go and stand behind your chairs."

"Pick up that paper."

"Fold up that oilcloth there."

"If you are playing instruments this morning and you haven't got your own recorder, make sure you've got them ready."
"You are playing the bells so go and stand by them ready. Remember to start on the bottom note."

"Michael, you give out the milk to your table, Jean to yours and Mary to yours."

No. 59. "Arrests attention by speaking to the children." 220

This is done by all the teachers, but not nearly to the same degree as in the two categories given above and it shows less variation as between teachers than do many other categories. Apparently all teachers need to use it sometimes but none very often. Averages are 4, 8 and 8.

The Nursery School study does not report this type of contact probably because the children are so seldom handled as a group during periods of free play.

"Children! Listen! Put the shops and houses which are newly painted not on the model, but on the shelf to dry."

"Just a minute! Who's got a rubber? Has anyone got a rubber to lend me?"

"Now children it is time for assembly. Leave what you are doing to go into the Hall."

H

No. 60. "Disapproves or discourages an action by words."   166

This category, though perhaps more negative than the others so far quoted, is hardly to be classified as reproof since, on the whole, it is the action rather than the child which is disapproved. Sometimes, however, it overlaps and comes very close to reproof as in the first example cited, though in the last it is entirely absent. Averages are 3 for teachers of five-year-olds and 7 for the other two groups. Teachers of five-year-olds do not appear to make much use of it and the Nursery School study does not give it at all.

EXAMPLES OF NO. 60

Boy (very subdued): "I broke the pot."
Teacher: "Oh, Peter, every time I ask you to wash something you break it."
(Peter looks very concerned.)
Teacher: "Go on. It can't be helped now. But you really must try to be more careful."

(To class): "Stop a minute, there's rather too much noise here."

To boy who is poking another with his instrument: "That is dangerous."

To a child who has modelled a chair: "It's a bit heavy, isn't it? I don't think it will stand up. I should try to do another tomorrow."

No. 61. "Disciplines by reproof."   145

Except for one teacher in each of the three age-groups, this occurs in the samples of every teacher but not very frequently. Averages are 4 for teachers of five-year-olds and 5 for the other two groups. As mentioned above, many of the "reproofs" are far from severe. The ratio given of only one severe reproof in the five examples quoted is, if anything, an over-estimate. There were few reproofs which carried that degree of blame.

In the Nursery School study N.36 is given as "Reproaches child for behaviour, untidiness or noise". Here, rather surprisingly, we have an average of 8 which is higher than any Infant School group of teachers, but as Miss Cass points out the "reproaches" are mostly very gentle and sometimes as in the example quoted later, almost playful.

EXAMPLES OF NO. 61 (Infant School Study)

Teacher: "Before you start I've got something to say to you — yesterday some children did woodwork but they were not very careful. They used the wood just as they found it and did not cut it down to the size they wanted and when they'd finished Miss — had to clear a lot of it away."

A hammer has been broken.
Teacher (to the child who did it): "I know you couldn't help breaking it, but you should have picked it up. You mustn't just leave it on the floor."

"Quieter boys! You are noisy lions!"

"You can enjoy your play without all this noise I think."

Clearing up time — one little girl still painting after instructions to clear up had been given.
Teacher: "Oh Wendy, I'm ashamed of you. It's packing up time. How can Peter clear up properly when you are doing that?"

No. 62. "Gives a warning that it is nearly time to clear up." 79

This is a sympathetic act to prevent later disappointment and give the children time to round off what they are doing before making a break. It appears in the records of twenty-three teachers. No score is above 6 for any teacher — averages are 3, 3 and 2. It falls into the group of contacts concerned with arresting attention.

It is not recorded in the Nursery School study probably because directives are seldom issued to whole classes and clearing up would be gradual and to some extent adjusted to individual children's readiness to stop, which would be influenced as they became aware that other children, assisted by teachers and helpers, were doing so.

EXAMPLES OF NO. 62

"Listen children, when you've finished the job you have finished, don't start anything else, clear your tables and see they are clean."

"Children, two more minutes and we shall have to clear."

Boy, wishing to begin some new work.
Teacher: "Well, we must start to think about that tomorrow as it is time to clear up now."

No. 63. "Stimulates by reproof."   68

This has been classified separately as the object here is clearly to produce greater effort and achievement rather than merely to reproach the child. It appears in the records of only four teachers of five-year-olds and five of six-year-olds, but is used by every teacher of the seven-year-olds. It is not very highly used. Only two teachers have records above 6 and twenty-three are under 3. It does not appear in the Nursery School study.

EXAMPLES OF No. 63

Child treads on the teacher's toe.
She says: "Oh Jim, what should you say?"
Boy: "Sorry, Miss Y."
Teacher: "There, you know what to say."

Teacher notices a boy standing about.
Teacher: "Get on! I don't know anyone who wastes as much time as you."

Teacher: "Michael, where are your models? You've been walking around with your hands in your pockets! Why don't you start your models?"
Boy: "All right."

No. 64. "Stimulates children by telling them to hurry."   (66 contacts)

Five of the teachers of five-year-old children have managed to avoid doing this in any of the sampled periods, but eight out of the ten teachers in each of the other two groups have records of it. While it is, no doubt, occasionally found to be desirable by teachers, especially of the older children, there is some evidence in the records that the teachers who do it most have external problems owing to the need to vacate rooms for other classes and conform to a time-table which almost certainly increases the number of times in which certain teachers have to hurry children more than they would otherwise do. The numbers are not high and average only 2 per teacher. It does not occur in the Nursery School records.

EXAMPLES OF NO. 64

Children are making book covers.
Teacher: "That's very well done. Just wipe off the surplus grease. See if you can hurry because I'm waiting for the press."

Girl making a dress for herself is slowly putting her frock on.
Teacher: "Hurry up and then I can go and help someone else."

Teacher goes out to the children doing woodwork: "Hurry up out there, you have a lot of clearing to do. Remember, every little bit has to be picked up."

Children making a model.
Teacher (to child sticking the grass): "Hurry up with the glue before it gets stiff again."

No. 65. "Arrests attention by clapping hands."   39

This only appears in the records of half the teachers and is not done very often except by two teachers who have records of 8 and 9, one of whom is mentioned as having a very quiet voice and a classroom much disturbed by the noise of traffic from the street. Two other teachers have records of 3 and 4 and the others are not above 2. Averages are 2 for teachers of five-year-olds and 0·5 and 1·5 for those of six and seven. It does not appear in the Nursery School records.

EXAMPLES OF NO. 65

Teacher: "Sh — ." (Claps her hands to gain the attention of the class.) "Children, will you start to clear away now."

Teacher claps her hands: "Everyone out now, please."

Teacher wishes to send some children to the Doctor — sorts the medical cards, claps her hands: "Children, listen a moment! I want these children to come to me."

No. 66. "Disciplines by her own example."   35

This is only recorded as occurring with seven of the teachers. Examples of this contact are not easily separated from other contacts and are shown in the teacher herself behaving as she has instructed or wishes the children to behave — for example, by standing or sitting quietly to await the signal to go to assembly, herself avoiding stepping on newly sown grass, etc.

It is not recorded in the Nursery School study.

No. 67. "Disciplines by isolating a child from others."   26

This is the first instance of punishment to appear in the records and it is perhaps the method most used when enlightened teachers of young children find it necessary to use punishment since there is a reasonableness involved in removing a child from those whom he has hurt or disturbed or sending an over-excited child out of the vicinity of others so as to give him time to calm down. It occurs in the records of only six teachers. It does not occur in the Nursery School

EXAMPLE

Teacher to child who has put clay in a little girl's hair who has protested: "Peter Jones, what are you doing? Go outside the door."

No. 68. "Stimulates by comparison."   21

This occurs in the records of eleven teachers. This contact, as is illustrated by the examples, is by no means always the rather dubious one of comparing one child's work or achievement with another. Sometimes the comparison is with an object or picture to encourage the child in his efforts to achieve reality and can hardly be regarded as "discipline". This category does not appear in the Nursery School records where it would no doubt be inappropriate to use it.

EXAMPLES OF NO. 68

Child: "Look, I've got paint on my dress."
Teacher: "You are careless. Look how clean Margaret has kept her frock." Gives the child some turpentine and says: "Try to clean it with this."

Child making a paper-maché cabbage.
Teacher: "I would make some outer leaves now. Cut your papers in half and stick round the outside just like cabbage leaves."

Girl making a puppet.
Teacher: "Do you want her to have fair hair or dark?"
Child: "Fair please."
Teacher (smiling): "Here's some lovely yellow wool. She'll have flaxen hair just like Cinderella" (in the picture).

MINOR CONTACTS

No. 69. "Arrests attention by asking the children to show their hands or some similar direction."   12

One teacher of five-year-olds uses this device seven times. Only five other teachers use it at all and have only one instance each. Nursery School teachers have no example of it.

No. 70. "Arrests attention by signals previously agreed upon with the children."   12

Only four teachers have any record. An example of this is a teacher who had arranged to say "One" when she wanted attention, hoping that "Two" or "Three" would then not be necessary. It is evident that most of the teachers rely more on the natural approach of simply telling the children when they want them to listen and are less inclined to rely on mechanical devices such as this or that of the previous category or clapping their hands. Again, this does not occur in the Nursery School records.

No. 71. "Shows disapproval by impatient movements."   10

Three teachers, one in each age-group, have one record of this and a fourth teacher of seven-year-olds has 7 instances. It is not recorded in the Nursery School study.

EXAMPLES OF NO. 71

Child (at woodwork bench): "Colin won't let me 'lend' (meaning borrow) his hammer."
Teacher (looking exasperated and jumping up quickly): "Dear me!" She goes out to the woodwork bench. "You'll have all to come in if you are going to be a nuisance."

At clearing up time child takes a pair of scissors.
Teacher (makes an impatient movement): "Here. I've just collected those. Put them back in the tin. You must finish tomorrow."

No. 72. "Disciplines by depriving the child of toys, tools, etc."   7

This is never recorded more than once for any one teacher. Five are teachers of seven-year-olds and only one is in each of the other age groups. It does not occur in the Nursery School study. It again illustrates how rarely these teachers find a need to use punishment and when they do what a reasonable form it takes.

EXAMPLES OF NO. 72

Children, looking at a beetle in a match box, crowding round are inclined to be fussy.
Teacher withdraws the box: "Children, you are being silly now. All the boys can look first."

A boy rings the little bell which is standing on the ledge. Teacher goes to bell and removes it to a high ledge.
Teacher (to the boy): "I'm sorry, I did ask you not to play with it."

No. 73. "Disapproves by glance or gesture."   (6 contacts)

This is only used by five of the teachers, and it does not occur in the Nursery School records. Examples are of a teacher who shakes her head at a group of children who are making too much noise and one who signals to a child in the playground who is teasing another child, to come indoors.

No. 74. "Arrests attention by raising voice."

One instance only from two teachers, illustrates how rarely the teachers need to raise their voices.

No. 75. "Ignores child deliberately."

Only occurs once in the records with a teacher of five-year-olds. There are, however, 19 records in the Nursery School study from the eighteen teachers of N.39, "Ignores a child's remark or action". It is sometimes wise with very young children, new to school, to allow behaviour which would be corrected with more experienced and secure children or to ignore the child who hopes to win attention by anti-social behaviour, provided the teacher gives such a child generous attention for other behaviour, which it is clearly evident that these good teachers are willing to do.

The Nursery School Study

N.34. "Reminds child of routine activity."   441

Example

Teacher: "Have you been to the toilet?" (Child shakes his head.) "Well, toilet first, please, or else you'll want to go in the middle of dinner."

N.35. "Gives a child a specific order."   339

Example

Teacher: "Bill, come off the table."

N.36. "Reproaches child for behaviour, untidiness or noise."   229

Example

Teacher: "Oh, Bobby, look at your legs! What have you been doing. You could do with a bath!"

N.37. "Refuses or deflects child's request for help, objects, attention or permission."   146

EXAMPLE

Child: "Can I come?"
Teacher: "No, dear, not just now. Doctor doesn't want to see you."

N.38. "Checks child's activity." 20

EXAMPLE

Teacher (taking toy gun): "We won't play with that now."

N.39. "Ignores child's remark or action." 19

EXAMPLE

Child: "Look at me, Miss X?" (Sticks a green paper shape on his nose.)
Teacher turns to another child and says: "Was it this book you wanted?"

N.40. "Rejects, suggests or reminds child of an acceptable form of behaviour." 5

EXAMPLE

Child: "I needn't have an apron on."
Teacher: "Yes, to keep your dungarees clean or you might get paint on them."

General comment on IIIC

The chief points which emerge are the unhesitating acceptance of these teachers of the rôle of leadership and their responsibility for guiding the child to good social behaviour and sensible attitudes towards work. It is also evident that they use positive approaches very much more than negative and make very little use of punishment. Reproofs, when used, are nearly always courteous and gentle and very often are accompanied by constructive advice. "Suggests and advises" is a very much used approach though there are plenty of positive commands on appropriate occasions.

As can be seen by comparison with Section IIIB, encouragement and praise are much more frequently used as a stimulus than reproof or reproach. There is a fairly consistent tendency throughout the categories for the teachers of children over six to give more commands and make more demand on the children's self control than do teachers of five-year-olds, which is natural since the older children are more securely established in school, more social and capable of greater achievement by standards of reality and more self-control.

GROUP IV

Actions of teachers when not in direct contact with the children of their own classes

This group of categories is obviously of less importance than the other three. Yet no picture of the teacher would be complete without the recognition that a teacher's time is very much distracted by administrative duties and by interruptions. One of the observers remarked that she thought that one of the marks of a good teacher was her ability to turn interruptions to good account, exploiting such situations for the benefit of the children. It has already been shown from certain examples how, for instance, the teachers use the checking of dinner and milk money as mathematical experience for the children. These categories, however, are of actions of the teacher which did not involve contact with her own class.

No. 76. "Chats to other adults or visitors including children from other classes."   366

As one would expect in informal Infant Schools, there is a certain amount of coming and going between classes. Children and teachers are often interested in the work going on in other classes and the

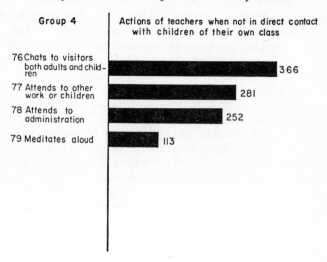

schools also attract a number of outside visitors. The teachers also had a few words sometimes with the observers. Every teacher in the sample has records of such contacts, the teachers of seven-year-olds having more, possibly because it is easier to leave the children for short periods than the more restive six-year-olds and under. Averages are 11, 10 and 16 for teachers of five-, six- and seven-year-olds.

The Nursery School teachers too have two categories, N.43, "Mentions child to another adult in the child's presence", and N.44, "Mentions child to another adult in the hearing of other children". There is also a category N.42, "Seeks adult co-operation, asks or gives information to adult". These categories all have small numbers and even when taken together, average only 2 contacts per teacher, but it must be remembered that these categories exclude the Infant School's wording "Chats". The Nursery School observers have confined themselves to recording matters of direct relevance to the children and the number of these is probably due largely to the presence of the Nursery Helpers. The figure is not really comparable with those of the Infant School study.

EXAMPLES OF No. 76 (Infant School Study)

Teacher asks observer to come and see boy's work. He is collecting foreign stamps. Teacher remarks to observer so that the boy can hear: "Don't you think he is a clever boy? He found Belgium all by himself and Malta and you know Malta is only like a little dot down there."

Headmistress enters and has a brief word with the teacher.

Teacher withdraws for a moment to speak to Welfare Officer.

Three boys are engaged in dramatic play.
Teacher turns to observer: "Just look at that. Aren't their positions excellent?"

A child comes in for the dinner money. Teacher holds her by both hands affectionately and says: "All right, Carol dear." She turns to observer and says, "Really, there's never any peace here."

No. 77. "Withdraws if necessary to attend to other business or other children." (281 episodes)

Here again every teacher has records of such withdrawals but in contrast to the last category, the teachers of seven-year-olds fall below those in the other age-groups, possibly because these older children are more capable of attending to some of the "other business" themselves. Averages are 11, 13 and 5 for teachers of five-, six- and seven-year-olds respectively. Again the Nursery School observers have not recorded.

EXAMPLES OF No. 77

Teacher picks up cleaning cloth, goes to cloakroom to wet the cloth. Returns and wipes all round the bin.

Teacher: "I've just remembered, I've got some water on." After few minutes she returns with jug of hot water which she pours into bath.

Miss X enters room and asks the teacher for something. Teacher, withdrawing for a moment, says, "Yes, certainly", and accedes to request.

No. 78. "Attends to administration." (252 episodes)

Two teachers of five-year-olds have no record of this, but all other teachers have scores. It is not recorded in the Nursery School study.

These records are concerned with registers, receiving and checking dinner money and the Doctor's visits.

No. 79. "Meditates aloud."   (113 instances)

Only four teachers have no record of doing this. It is an interesting facet of the characteristics of the teachers, who spend so much time talking to the children, that they nearly all at times feel a need to talk to themselves. It is not done very frequently, but it is very widespread and gives evidence that the teachers felt at ease in the presence of the observers. Comments are usually brief or relevant to what is going on at the time. Averages are, 3, 3 and 5 for teachers of five-, six- and seven-year-olds respectively.

The Nursery School study too has the same category (N.41) and only four of their eighteen teachers have no record of doing it. Their proportional average is 5 which brings them up to the average for teachers of seven-year-olds, and higher than in the other Infant School age-groups. Moreover, the Nursery School study has another category N.45, "Exclamations used by the teacher", which in the Infant School study would probably be included in No. 79. There are only 10 episodes under N.45 which would raise the Nursery School average to 5·5 if added to 41. The Nursery School example quoted for N.45 seems ambiguous but had it been said to the child rather than the teacher to herself it would no doubt have been classified as "Gives sympathy and comfort".

EXAMPLES OF No. 79 (Infant School Study)

All the following remarks were made by the teacher to herself:
"Ah, I thought that would happen!"
"Now who was I looking for to help?"
"I wonder if I have one anywhere."
"I shall be very cross if they don't soak those brushes."
"Now let me see if this is long enough."

THE NURSERY SCHOOL STUDY

	Total no. of instances from 18 teachers
N.41. "Meditates aloud."	155

EXAMPLE

Teacher: "Oh, I wonder where it can be?" (A lost piece of a puzzle.)

N.42. "Seeks adult co-operation, asks or gives information to adult." 27

EXAMPLE

Teacher (to helper): "Will you go and get Jill quickly. Her leg is stuck."

N.43. "Mentions child to adult in child's presence." 18

EXAMPLE

Teacher (to helper): "That's Lindy's basket. Go and hang it on her peg."

N.44. "Mentions child to adult in the hearing of other children." 15

EXAMPLE

Teacher (to helper): "Willie's made London Airport."

N.45. "Exclamations used by the teacher." 10

EXAMPLE

Child: "Her head's come off" (referring to paper doll).
Teacher: "Oh, what a shame!"

CHAPTER V

Further examination of evidence revealed by the records

EXAMINATION of the total number of contacts made by the Infant School teachers reveals that those concerned with the imparting of information and the provision of intellectual stimulus (Group I) are the most numerous, though they are not far ahead of those in Group III which are described as being concerned with establishing a setting which is favourable to education and which are of equal importance to the child's emotional, social and intellectual welfare. Even if one omitted the contacts of "observation", leaving only those concerned with praise and encouragement, discipline and control, this group still comes well above Group II where the contacts are particularly concerned with fostering and encouraging good social attitudes.

In the Nursery School study, however, this Group II comes highest though it is fairly closely followed by Group I (the intellectual contacts), whereas the Group III contacts come lower.*

It is possible that this difference in emphasis is appropriate to the stage of development of the children in Nursery Schools as compared with those in Infant Schools. For example, with very young children the need for direct and personal expression of affection by the teacher is often very great whereas older children are often most aware of the teacher's affection when she praises their work or enters with sympathy into their intellectual interests or helps them solve a problem. Younger children too need more direct help in making social contacts with other children and the Infant School's No. 34, "Promotes social attitudes between children or considerate be-

* Infant School Study — Total number of contacts
      Group I   6672
      Group II 3401
      Group III (less observation) 5196

  Nursery School Study
      Group II 4681
      Group I   4460
      Group III (observation not recorded) 2833

haviour", is much lower than the Nursery School N.20 which deals with the same matter.

It is clear that the Infant School teachers are by no means indifferent to the importance of helping children in this way, since 151 incidences of it have been recorded, but it appears that the need for it is less at an age when children have had considerable experience of playing and working with other children.

It is also worth noting how very high the "intellectual" contacts are in the Nursery School study — good evidence, if any is still needed, that a trained Nursery School teacher is more than a "child minder". It should also be noted that there is no use of punishment in the Nursery School records nor of any "tricks" or devices for maintaining order or arresting attention. These are also very low in the Infant School study despite the handicap to the Infant School teacher of having to guide large classes without any additional helpers.

Variation and similarity of techniques used by different teachers

No two teachers, of course, used precisely similar techniques and in almost all the categories recorded there is a considerable divergence in the scores of different teachers. A histogram was made for each type of contact showing the number of times it appeared in the records of each teacher and this device made it simple to trace the contacts which showed a greater or lesser degree of variation between the use of them by different teachers.

The techniques which showed least difference are listed below since they show the features most common to all the teachers.

1. *Used by all, or nearly all, the teachers to a high degree*
   Helps by producing material.
   Assents by word or gesture.
   Praises child's performance, work or action.
   Suggests or advises appropriate action or behaviour.

2. *Used by all, or nearly all, the teachers but to a less high degree*
   Gives information or explanation in answer to a question.
   Helps by demonstrating skill.
   Helps by directing the use of material.
   Helps by indicating the whereabouts of material.
   Helps by suggesting the use of material.
   Comforts and reassures by speaking to a child.

I

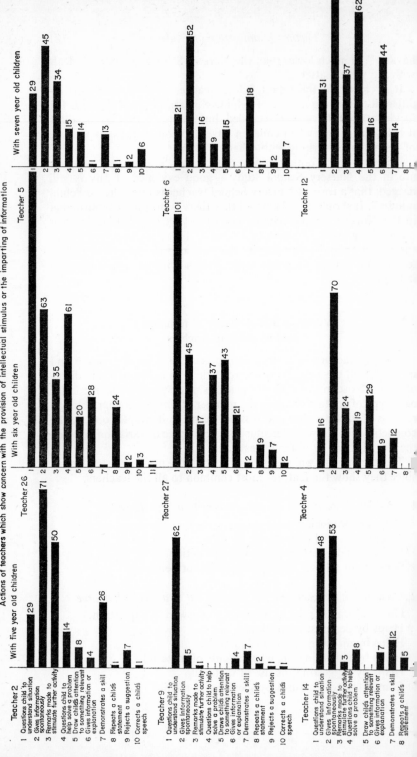

Comparison of nine teachers showing variation of contacts in group IA

Actions of teachers which show concern with the provision of intellectual stimulus or the imparting of information

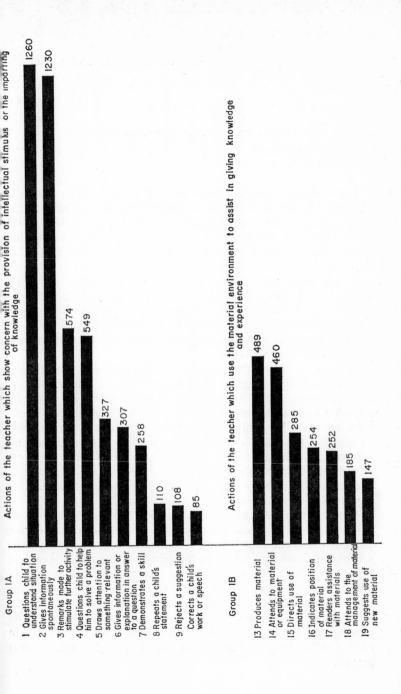

Actions of the teacher which show concern with the provision of intellectual stimulus or the imparting of knowledge

Group 1A

1 Questions child to understand situation — 1260
2 Gives information spontaneously — 1230
3 Remarks made to stimulate further activity — 574
4 Questions child to help him to solve a problem — 549
5 Draws attention to something relevant — 327
6 Gives information or explanation in answer to a question — 307
7 Demonstrates a skill — 258
8 Repeats a child's statement — 110
9 Rejects a suggestion — 108
Corrects a child's work or speech — 85

Actions of the teacher which use the material environment to assist in giving knowledge and experience

Group 1B

13 Produces material — 489
14 Attends to material or equipment — 460
15 Directs use of material — 285
16 Indicates position of material — 254
17 Renders assistance with materials — 252
18 Attends to the management of material — 185
19 Suggests use of new material — 147

Makes a promise to a child.

Enlists co-operating between the child and herself.

Directs or encourages children to co-operate and enlists co-operation between children.

Thanks a child.

Arrests attention by speaking to a child.

3. *Used seldom but by nearly all the teachers on occasions*

Rejects a suggestion.

Meditates aloud.

The contacts, which are much more numerous, which show the characteristic variation as between different teachers reveal not that good teachers differ fundamentally in what they are seeking to do for children, but that they tend to adopt different ways of achieving their purposes. The high number of scores in all the groups of contacts when examined as a whole shows clearly that all the teachers were concerned with adding to the child's knowledge and skill, promoting his power of thinking and reasoning, fostering friendly relationships between children and helpful social behaviour and were also concerned with the child's values and the development of good traits of character also that they were warm and friendly in their relations with the children.

Sometimes it is clear that a teacher who does not make much use of one way of, for example, encouraging thought and reasoning, tends to "compensate" by making more use of others. For example, a teacher who has no score on "Draws the child's attention to something relevant" has a high one on "Helps by questioning the child to help him towards the solution of a problem or towards gaining further information" and a good many teachers who have low records on "Helps by giving information or explanation in answer to a question" come very high on "Helps by giving information or explanation spontaneously".

However, there are also some examples of consistency throughout a whole group of contacts, showing a different balance in the particular gifts and contribution of individual teachers so that while no teacher is without scores in the whole of any group some are lower throughout a whole group and sometimes higher in another group than other teachers are. Some teachers of five-year-olds, for example, are rather lower than some of the other teachers in Group IA ("intellectual" contacts) while some of these "compensate" by making more use of the organisation and presentation of material to aid the child's learning (Group IB), others are higher still in other groups.

Some teachers show a similar consistency in high scores throughout most of the items in a whole group, as for example the teacher who came highest of all the teachers in giving comfort both by words and by caress is also high, (though not actually the highest) in "attention to the child's clothing and physical comfort".

On the whole the purely social contacts between teacher and child tend to show the greatest consistency, as if some teachers tend to show their concern with the child more directly than others do, but there are examples of "compensation" in this group also, as for example, a teacher who has no record of "greeting a child" has a high score on "chatting to a child".

The group concerned with discipline and control also shows that it is not possible to claim that all teachers "compensate" for not using one type of direct leadership by using more of another, though there is a tendency in the first two contacts "Suggests and advises" and "Gives a direct command" for teachers to use one of these methods at the expense possibly of the other. However, even here there is no exact uniformity since though the teacher who comes highest on "Suggests and advises" is lower than most other teachers on giving direct commands, the teacher who is lowest on using direct commands is not very high on "Suggests and advises".

It is true, on the whole, to say that the evidence suggests that teachers obtain their good results by widely differing means. Some seem to achieve discipline by a close and friendly relationship with each child, very much more than by direct exercise of leadership, and others by particular attention to intellectual stimulus, good organisation and encouragement of the child's work and effort.

It is perhaps relevant here to recall that contacts in which all teachers tend to score highly include the production of material and praise and encouragement of the child's performance, work or action, though "Suggests and advises" is also very high.

Differences in the techniques used by teachers of different age-groups in the Infant School

Since, unlike the Nursery Schools, the Infant School classes used in this study were for children of similar chronological ages, I had the opportunity of noting differences in the proportion of contacts made by teachers working with different age-groups. Numbers are too small to enable me to draw definite conclusions but since some of the differences found seemed possibly to reflect the differing characteristics of children during a period when rapid development is taking place, I decided to obtain additional evidence by devoting two years to collecting evidence in many more classes of the purposes for which children of these ages sought the teacher. This evidence is given in the following section.

The most striking indications of differences as shown in the above records, which I hoped to check by the further study, are as follows:

The strongly shown increase in nearly every category in Group IA of numbers as between the ages of five and six seem to indicate that at the age of six the child demands considerably more of his teacher in the matter of imparting information and helping him to achieve skill. If the average numbers of each contact in Group IA are added, a total is shown of

120 for teachers of five-year-olds
178 for teachers of six-year-olds
and 181 for teachers of seven-year-olds

The rise between six and seven is very much less than between five and six.

Contacts in which the rise at six is most important are: Nos. 1, 2, 4, 5 and 6. Only in one contact does six come lower than five and that is No. 7, "Helps by demonstrating skill". The only contact in which a rise is considerably greater between six and seven than between five and six is No. 3, "Remarks made with the sole object of stimulating further activity".

It seemed, therefore, desirable to try to check the hypothesis that children aged six and over seek the teacher more frequently for information and intellectual help than do children of five. In Group IB, where the teacher is using material to aid her teaching, there is, however, no rise at six, in fact the total average scores are lower at this age than either at five or seven (63, 55 and 70 respectively). Differences are not very large and may well be insignificant, but it seemed worth trying to check whether the seven-year-old is more concerned than the six-year-old with correct use of material and so demands more help from his teacher in that way. That the five-year-old needs more help than the six-year-old in the matter of finding material and in its arrangement and management is probably self-evident.

Group IIA ("Actions of rendering physical care, protection or comfort") as was to be expected, shows a higher number of five-year-old contacts and the numbers drop as the child grows older and more competent and also more secure in the school situation. Average totals are 28, 13 and 8 for the respective age-groups. In Group IIB (personal friendly contacts from teacher to child) the teachers of six-year-olds fall slightly below either those of five or seven, but the numbers may be insignificant (52, 45 and 52).

In Group IIC (Actions of the teacher which show concern with promoting social attitudes) the total average scores — 51, 51 and 44 — are slightly misleading since they include both instances when the teacher asks the child for help, which is rather more frequently done with six than with five-year-olds (26, 29, 28) and instances of directing or assisting children to co-operate with each other where, as one would expect, the average is higher in teachers of five-year-olds (17, 13, 12).

In Group IIIA (observes the children) there is an interesting drop at six caused by the categories of the teacher observing without comment which has been referred to above and which may indicate that while it is not so difficult for a teacher to understand what the child is doing or wanting when he is six as when he is five, the six-year-old needs to have comments made at the time rather than saved up for a discussion period, which the observers noted was sometimes done by teachers of seven-year-olds. Averages are 28, 18 and 36. It is, unfortunately, not possible to examine the above hypothesis by analysing for what purposes the children actively seek the teacher except that part of it might perhaps be suggested by six-year-olds coming more frequently than seven-year-olds for comment on or approval of their work.

In Group IIIB (Praise and encouragement) the figures rise slightly between six and seven but by a larger amount from five to six. However, it should be noted that by far the largest number of categories were concerned with praise or encouragement of the child's work and achievements. Where praise of more personal matters are concerned, i.e. the child's gift and the child's appearance, the five-year-olds' teachers have an average of 9 as against 1 each in the other two groups.

In Group IIIC (Discipline and control) there are considerably fewer instances in the records of the teachers of five-year-olds, a total average of 65 as compared with 103 and 100 with teachers of six and seven-year-olds. It seems that teachers of five-year-olds, like the Nursery School teachers, are able to maintain discipline more by indirect means. Like the Nursery School records there is no instance among teachers of five-year-olds of the use of punishment.

Results of the two years' further study

The object of undertaking this work (with consequent delay in publication of the results of the whole enquiry) was that it seemed to be of considerable interest and value to know whether the differences in the number of certain types of contact which appeared in the records of teachers of children of one age, as compared with those of another, were in fact caused by differences in the children's stages of development, rather than merely by the teachers' assumption that their function ought to change as the children grew older. Knowing the sensitivity of good Infant School teachers to the real needs of children, I felt it was probable that the differences did reflect changing attitudes in the children, but it seemed wise to devise a procedure which allowed us to observe the children rather than the teacher, and also to add to the number of classes in which observations were made — since ten classes of each age were not very many. During the two years following the compilation of the first results, it was necessary to use additional schools and the delay gave us the opportunity to interview and observe the work of more teachers, also, of course, of the same quality as those who were observed in the first enquiry.

It was found possible to observe the children in eighteen classes for four periods of one hour in each class, making a record of every purpose for which a child sought the teacher. This eliminated the possibility that it was the teacher who chose to give help of one kind rather than another, so that if these records provided confirmation of the opinions expressed in the previous section, I felt I should be on firmer ground in assuming that children in the different age-groups had different needs in certain respects. Six classes of approximately forty children in each, were observed in each of the three age-groups. Allowing for the absences of certain children during the days when the samples were taken, it may be said that the following table represents the approaches made to the teacher during four hours, in periods when children were free to choose their own occupations, by approximately 200 children of five years old in six different classes, and the same number of children and of classes of six- and seven-year-olds respectively, about 600 children in all. Four hours of observation were made on four different days in each classroom and a note taken of any child who sought the teacher for any purpose. On some occasions, when the child was not audible, we asked the teacher, who then told us for what the child had come.

Table of contacts made about 200 children of five, 200 of six and 200 of seven years old during four hours of recording in each classroom. The children were in eighteen different classes.

	Children aged		
	5	*6*	*7*
Ia For comfort and reassurance	14	11	5
Ib For support against other children	71	60	41
Ic For help in managing clothes	78	22	10
Id For help in finding belongings	4	8	4
	167	101	60

These contacts are clearly for the purpose of seeking personal comfort and care and, as might be expected, show a larger number at the age of five followed by a steady drop to seven.

	Children aged		
	5	6	7
Ie To ask permission to do something	331	309	170
If ,, ,, where to put things	37	19	22

These two contacts which show dependence upon the teacher in the matter of classroom activities, show a less marked difference except in the greater independence of seven-year-olds in Ie.

	Children aged		
	5	6	7
IIa For help with reading	15	44	39
IIb ,, ,, ,, spelling	34	183	129
IIc ,, ,, ,, creative work	63	39	96
IId ,, ,, ,, other work (tasks such as weighing, compiling charts and fixing constructional toys)	44	64	63
IIe To ask for materials or tools	105	115	135
IIf ,, ,, ,, information	72	58	83
	333	503	545

The totals show the expected rise between five and six but the differences in this group are not as marked as might have been expected from the records of the teachers' contacts. They do however show consistency with them in the tendency of six-year-olds to ask for less help in creative work, which again suggests that they need less help than the five-year-olds in managing material but are less concerned than the seven-year-old in achieving standards of a realistic or accurate nature, and so are less inclined to feel the need for help in this respect. In other forms of "work" they ask for more help than the five-year-olds, but do not seek information more often. If the group of contacts is treated as a whole as representing the seeking of aid from the teacher in the matter of classroom "work" the seven-year-olds are higher than either of the other age groups though six is higher than five. The six-year-olds no doubt seek more help with reading because they need it more than the seven-year-olds, whereas the five-year-olds would engage in reading less frequently in a period of free choice. The increase in requests for help with spelling also shows a rise at six.

	Children aged		
	5	6	7
IIIa For appreciation of creative work	245	233	220
IIIb ,, ,, ,, ideas	45	81	22
IIIc ,, ,, ,, other work	71	183	110
	361	497	352

The six-year-olds appear to be very eager for appreciation of their ideas and for much of their other work also.

	Children aged		
	5	6	7
IVa To tell about their families	17	5	7
IVb ,, ,, ,, themselves and their doings	65	39	22
IVc ,, ,, ,, their clothes	19	6	4
IVd ,, ,, ,, things other children are doing	54	32	22
IVe ,, give information arising from thought or reasoning	14	12	29

IVe is clearly of a different nature from the other motives which lead children to talk to the teacher. It is more concerned with exchange of thoughts and shows a rise at the age of seven. The other motives, which are much more personal, show the highest total scores at five and the lowest at seven.

	Children aged		
	5	6	7
Va To show affection for the teacher	14	1	7
Vb ,, give something to the teacher	50	15	23
Vc ,, help the teacher	36	17	18
Vd ,, share a joke or humorous situation with the teacher	32	12	11
Ve ,, show or tell the teacher something with the main motive of interesting her	160	99	138
	292	144	197

This result confirms one of the predictions I made before examining the results, that the six-year-olds would appear to be less demonstrative towards the teacher than either of the other age-groups and would seek fewer of such personal contacts but more for approval of their work. It is interesting that they have very considerably more contacts with the teacher for approval of their work, and ideas (see Section III) than for more directly personal motives. The proportional difference is considerably less at five and at seven. Other predictions which are suggestively confirmed are that:

1. The seven-year-old will be more concerned with the *correct* use of material than the six-year-old.
2. Five-year-olds will seek more personal care and comfort and protection than older children will do.
3. Five-year-olds will also seek more help in managing materials.

A prediction which is *not* confirmed by this evidence was that six-year-olds will seek the teacher more frequently for information than do five-year-olds. The seven-year-olds ask for the most information but the five-year-olds come next and six-year-olds lowest.

Other points which possibly throw light of developmental differences in the ages from five to seven are:

1. The greater ability of the children as they pass through the period to manage their relations with other children without the support of the teacher.
2. The growing confidence and independence which enables seven-year-olds not to need to ask permission so frequently. The teachers sometimes commented on the fact that six-year-olds often asked quite unnecessarily and probably more for approval of their intentions than in doubt as to whether permission would be withheld. It may well be further evidence of their wish to have their ideas approved of.
3. The tendency to be demonstrative towards the teacher, though strongest at five, shows a rise at seven over six which confirmed Gesell's description of the seven-year-old's frequent feelings of affection for the teacher. The eagerness of the six-year-old for approval also reflects his statement that "Praise is elixir to the six-year-old", and there is perhaps also an indication that confirms his picture of the "tougher" behaviour of the six-year-olds, in the rise at six of the contacts of the teacher which show positive measures for winning the child's co-operation, i.e. "Stimulates by encouragement; enlists co-operation between the child and herself, praises the child's performance, work or action and thanks the child." These are all ways in which good teachers seek to win co-operation rather than by reproof.

Analysis of the teaching given in free choice periods under "Subjects" of the school curriculum

Much of the informal and incidental teaching given in free choice periods dealt with material which in former days might have been imparted to children by means of formal "lessons", talks given by the teacher or in very early days by "object" lessons. It seemed of value to undertake the somewhat laborious task of working through the sampled records of at least some of the teachers to discover how much information of a kind which might fall under "subject" categories was in fact being given by teachers in informal ways in relation to the children's spontaneous interests. Owing to the enthusiasm of one of the observers we were able to analyse the records of nineteen of the teachers. The table of total contacts is given below. The two largest categories are

Mathematics 149 contacts
and English   86   ,,

These have been sub-divided since they both are broad subjects which involve several different kinds of teaching.

Mathematics

Here the teaching given involved help with understanding

Money	41 episodes
Measuring	30 ,,
Number	29 ,,
Weighing	16 ,,
Spatial relationships or "Geometry"	13 ,,
Time	11 ,,
Fractions	5 ,,
Multiplication	2 ,,
Capacity	1 ,,

English is sub-divided as follows

Reading	37 episodes
Language	22 ,,
Writing	12 ,,
Dramatic work	7 ,,
Spelling	7 ,,
Poetry	1 ,,

It should be noted that the schools used for this analysis were ones in which the period for free play was separated from those in which the children normally expected to be engaged in the activities of reading, writing or arithmetic, otherwise no doubt the numbers of all these contacts would come much higher.

Other "subjects" occur in the following order:

Handicraft	56 episodes
General knowledge	42 ,,
Geography	33 ,,
Biology (animals)	29 ,,
Needlework	24 ,,
Science (non-biological)	18 ,,
Domestic Science and Homecraft	15 ,,
Biology (plants)	14 ,,
Art	11 ,,
Music	9 ,,
Health education	8 ,,
Physical education	7 ,,
History	5 ,,
Divinity	3 ,,

A few examples are given to illustrate the type of episode which has been assigned to "Subject" categories. Of course, much of the help given by teachers could not be so assigned. As the observer who made the analysis remarks "It would be extremely interesting to note those contacts which helped the child's social development." This was very evident in the younger age-groups where the "intellectual" contacts were fewer. She also comments on the fact that it was very probable that the teachers fostered many of the interests by further questions or information outside the periods which were recorded and that her attempt to assign episodes to subject divisions are only tentative, but that at least her work did indicate the wide range of children's interests at this early age.

EXAMPLES

MATHEMATICS: MONEY

Child counting money

T. "Can you do something for me?" (Takes purse out of handbag.) "Can you count out 8/-?"
    (Child counts out 8/-.)
T. "Good — Well done!"

Child and teacher with toy shop

T. "Leonard, here are 10 pennies. What would you like today?"
C. "An aeroplane please."

T. "Aeroplanes cost 6*d*."
    (C. gives teacher 6*d*.)
T. "How much have you left? Lets count and then we shall know."

MATHEMATICS: TIME

Children with puppets

T. "What time is the puppet show? What time does the clock say?"
C. "12.15." (Teacher watches children writing.)
T. "That says 12. How will you make it say 12.15?"

Child talking to teacher

C. "I have a real watch at home. I can tell the time."
T. "Can you? I'd like to know what time it is now. Will you go and look?"

NUMBER

Child modelling a dog

T. "Are those enough legs?"
    (Child shakes head.)
T. "How many have you got?"
C. "Two."

Girl knitting

T. "You've got 8 stitches on. How many more do I need to put on? Yes, that's right, 12. . . . Count these and make sure there are 20."
C. "19."
T. "There may only be 19. You check as well, Brenda."

Child with knitting

C. "Miss X is my knitting 3 inches yet?"
T. "Well, we'll see. Fetch me a ruler, Jean."
C. "Where the 3 inch mark, Miss X?"
T. "Count it, dear. Now put the ruler at the bottom of your knitting and measure up."
C. "It's only 2 inches so I have another inch to do."

Boy making a boat

T. "Can you have some cloth for a sail?" (repeating child's statement). "Did you measure how long you wanted it?"
C. "21 inches."
T. "How many feet and inches is that?" (Helps child to work it out.)

GEOMETRY

Children at junk table making the Dome of Discovery

T. "I don't think you can manage to cut a circle without something to give you the shape."

C.1. "A big plate will do."
C.2. "We need three tins the same size and there are only two."
C.3. "They could saw this in half."

Boy making boat

T. "How wide do you want it at the bottom? What shape do you want it to be? Go and get a piece of paper and draw the shape you want."
(Child brings drawing of sail.)
T. "This side has to be straight. Now you want a straight bit of sail down there. Do you know what that shape is called?"
(Child replies.)
T. "That's right, a triangle."

WEIGHING

Two girls who are cooking

T. (referring to scales) "I'll look. It just went down didn't it. Now what do you weigh next? Look at the card." (Recipes pinned to wall) "Yes — 4 oz of fat. Don't forget to change the weight."

Child weighing

T. "How many ounces in $\frac{1}{4}$ lb of lentils."
C. "Four."
T. "Now you've got to weigh 4 oz."
(C. finds weights.)
T. "Yes, that's right."

MULTIPLICATION

Child in home corner, pretends to be milkman

C. "I've only got one bottle left and I've got a whole street to do."
T. "What will you do?"
C. "Get two more crates."
T. "Then how many will you have?"
C. "I don't know."
T. "Go and count the bottles in one of our milk crates."
C. "24."
T. "Then you would need 2 times 24. How many?"
C. "48."

Child with packet of coconut

C. "I have 4 oz of coconut so I can make 4 times as many cakes."
T. "I think if you make twice the quantity that will be enough. Before you begin to mix it, write out your recipe using 2 times as much of everything and let me see it."

CAPACITY

Child at water table

C. "Miss Y, what is a gill?"
T. "It's a quarter of a pint, dear."

SPATIAL RELATIONSHIPS

Child doing potato printing

T. "Do you want a space or not?"
C. "A space."
T. "Well put the ruler where you want it. I'd like you to do it all yourself."

Child in home corner

(Teacher goes to house and sees too many children there.)
T. "Do you think we could make the house bigger, like this? Then more people can play in it." (Pulls walls of house out to extend size.)

FRACTIONS

Child with waste material making a house

C. "I want to put a roof on this house."
T. "How are you going to do it?"
C. "I don't know."
T. "Shall I show you? Here is some beautiful red paper. First we fold it in half, then measure it beside your house."

Boy cutting cakes

T. "Cut them exactly in half. You are cutting yours into quarters Steven. Charles is cutting his in half. Make them all the same size."

ENGLISH: READING

Child with picture

T. "Would you like me to write about it?"
C. "Yes."
(Teacher writes and speaks each word as she writes.)

Child with knitting pattern

C. "Mrs. C. — we're going to do this."
T. "Find out how many stitches you will need."
C. "Points out number on pattern."
T. "Is that the number of stitches? You read what it says."

LANGUAGE

Child with sellotape

C. "Can I lend the sellotape?"
T. "You don't mean lend. *I* am going to lend it to *you*. You are going to borrow it."

Children cooking

C. "Come and see the cakes now. We have mixed them."
T. "They are just the right consistency. Do you know what that word means? Neither too soft nor too stiff. Just right."

WRITING

Child with picture

C. "Will you show me how to write my name on it?"
  (Teacher writes on card.)
T. "Now you copy it. You can keep this card and then you can use it again."

Child with crayoning picture

T. "Shall I write 'bread van'? Are you going to write it on your picture now?"
C. "Yes."

DRAMATIC WORK

Teacher to performers

T. "Well, how are you getting on?"
C. "All right but they won't listen to me."
T. "You must listen to the Ringmaster, he is there to help you."

Children acting "Jack and the Beanstalk"

T. "Now I'm going to watch this play. Are you ready to show me?"
C. "We've started."
T. "Will you start again so that I can see it from the beginning? You'll have to speak louder. There's a noise here and one next door so call out. . . ."

SPELLING

Child talking to teacher

C. "I want to put a word in my dictionary but I can't spell it."
T. "What is it?"
C. "The word 'straight'."
T. (writing word) "There you are. It's a hard word."

Child writing story

C. "Will you write 'spring'?"
T. "I think you could write it on your own. Try. What does it begin with?"
C. "S."
  (Teacher nods.)
T. "What comes next?"
C. "P.R.I."
T. (repeating) "Yes — P.R.I. — then what?"
  (Child hesitates.)
T. "N.G."

POETRY

Child reciting a hymn

T. "Shall I show you how I would say that?"
  (Teacher reads.)
T. "What's the difference between the way you read it and the way I've read it?"
C. "You say it in a quiet voice and your face smiles."

K

ART

Child sewing

T. "Lay your needlework on the table and see which colour you think looks nice. You could choose two colours and we could make a flower like this." (The child experiments with colours.)

Child painting

(Child has just discovered that red and yellow make orange.)

T. "Isn't it interesting to find which colour we get when we mix two together. I should try mixing yellow and blue next. Come and tell me what they make."

HOUSECRAFT

Child washing

(Child fetches washing bowl.)

T. "Let me show you how to wash." (Demonstrates.)

Children washing

T. "I think I should rinse them once more if I were you."

(To child): "You've been helping to get the clothes clean haven't you? Have you finished washing?"

NEEDLEWORK

Child sewing

T. "What stitch do you want to do?"

C. "Slanting stitch."

T. "This is how you do it." (Demonstrates.)

Children with sacks

C. "Here are the sacks. We're going to make Red Indian suits."

T. "Lay them flat on the table and with chalk, make the shape of the trousers."

DIVINITY

Child with prayer book

T. "Miss X said would you like to read the first four pages of your prayers. Have you got your book with prayers in. Go into a corner and practise reading it in a nice big voice."

Children practising a play

C. "What does the innkeeper do?"

T. "He takes the lantern and shows Mary and Joseph the shed."

HISTORY

Child making castle

C. "Miss B — look at my castle."
T. "It's lovely — which castle is it?"
C. "Windsor."
T. "Bring that red book to me. Here is a picture of Windsor Castle."

Discussion

T. "What does History mean?"
C. "About the early days."

MUSIC

Child in music corner

C. "Miss F, I can play a tune."
T. "Can you! Let me hear you."
    (Child plays scale.)
T. "That's right. If you read the letters on the chime bars you'll see that they
    go like the alphabet. What do you notice about the size. . . . Yes —
    they're different. Which are the big ones?"
C. "The low notes."

Four children in the music corner

T. "I'm going to play something and get you to answer me. Now play it
    again and make up your own answer."

PHYSICAL EDUCATION

Child skipping

    (Teacher takes rope from the girl.)
T. "Now we can skip." (Demonstrates.)

Child jumping

C. "Watch me jump off the table."
T. "That's very good."

GEOGRAPHY

Child with stamp

C. "This is a South African stamp, and we only have an African page."
T. "That's all right dear, put it on the same page."
    (Teacher picks up pencil.)
"If this was Africa, the top would be called North and the bottom South,
but they would still be Africa."

Boy at woodwork

C. "Look at my chopper."
T. "It looks like a tomahawk. In the book of Red Indians in the library,
    you'll find a picture of a tomahawk."

BIOLOGY: PLANTS

Child to teacher at Nature Table

C. (looking at crocuses) "I like looking for the yellow things you showed us."
T. "Do you mean the stamens."
C. "Yes, that's it — with the pollen on."

Boy talking to teacher

C. "My nasturtiums have green things on top."
T. "They're the little shoots coming out. Why do they bend forward. Do you know?"
C. "No."
T. "They bend towards the light."

BIOLOGY: ANIMALS

Children with mice

T. "You've got them all muddled up. Now we shall be having families. Let me put the two men together. You see we don't want them to have babies in the holidays. Let me see if this is Mrs. White."

Two children with hamster

T. "You watch. He's going to put all the food in his pouch and take it up to his bed."

HEALTH EDUCATION

Teacher to children

T. "Will all the children who have handled the guinea pigs, please wash your hands."

Children in home corner

T. "How your baby has grown. You must feed her well. What do you use?"
C. "Cow and Gate."

DOMESTIC SCIENCE

Children cooking

C. "Mrs. — our dough is too wet."
T. "Is it?" (Adds more flour.) "Oh it *is* sticky, isn't it! If you keep it well floured it won't stick to the board."

Child cooking

C. "What do you put in first, currants or flour or milk?"
T. "What are you making?"
C. "Scones."
T. "Put the flour in first."

CRAFT

Boy with sword

C. "I made this last night."
T. "What are you going to do about this" (pointing to the end).
C. "Make it smooth."
T. "Before you do that, I should make it level. If you look in the reference book, you would find out how to decorate a sword."

Child with tool

C. "This isn't a screw driver is it?"
T. "No, a gimlet."

Child making scooter

C. "Miss Y, will you give me some smaller nails?"
T. "You really want staples. Hold the scooter and I'll place them in position."

SCIENCE: NON-BIOLOGICAL

Teacher at water trough

T. "I wonder why the pebbles have gone to the bottom and the cork is floating on the top?"
   (C. looks puzzled.)
T. "Because stones are heavy so they sink. Cork is always light and that's why it floats."

Children with toy trains

C. "Wouldn't it be nice if real smoke came out of the engine."
T. "You mean steam, dear. Do you know what makes the steam?"
C. "The fire in the engine. It boils up the water and makes steam."
T. "Yes, that's right, then the steam comes out of the funnel at the top. Its the steam that makes the engine go."

GENERAL KNOWLEDGE

Child with box

T. "What's this?"
C. "An archway."
T. "What goes under archways."
C. "Trains sometimes, and buses."

Boy making boat

T. "What sort of ship are you making, John?"
C. "A sailing boat."
T. "What are you going to make the sails from?"
C. "I was going to use newspaper."
T. "Could you think of anything else?"
C. "Cloth would be better."

Child with model of church

C. "Isn't that part called the spire?"

T. "Can you tell me what else churches are famous for?"

C. "Windows."

T. "Yes. Why are some church windows so lovely?"

C. "Because they are made of pretty glass."

T. "Yes. We usually say stained glass."

CHAPTER VI

Aspects of the teachers' work which are relevant to informal teaching, but on which evidence cannot be obtained by samples taken during periods of free occupation

A. **Examination of the question of how far the teacher encourages or gives opportunity for the children to carry over interests from the free choice period into periods devoted to other subjects or how far interests established during other periods influence the children's activities in the free choice time.**

The techniques necessary to obtain this information were two-fold. Teachers were observed on several occasions throughout the whole day and were interviewed on the subject, care being taken not to imply that such links *ought* to be made, but merely that we were interested in whether they did happen to occur or not. The teachers' answers were found to confirm on the whole what had been observed and the observations were made before the interviews were held. There were, however, some examples given quite fully by teachers of how they had followed up certain happenings at times when observers had not been present and it was clear that the evidence would have been more scanty if observations alone had been used. We should also have lost the significance of our observed "follow up" activities of the teacher because we would not have seen the events which led the teacher to take them up later.

The following remarks apply to a sample of thirty teachers which was as many as we were able to study in this connection. In three cases only were there no links at all and the free choice period appeared to be quite isolated from what the children did during the rest of the day. In seven more cases the reports are "very little". To find a third of the teachers in these two groups was somewhat disappointing and one wonders whether there is not room for more exploration, even by good teachers, of the possibilities of providing for the extension of the purposes and interests of the children into other times of the daily programme. That the teachers were not unaware of the link between the children's play and the subjects of the curriculum is shown in the previous chapter by the large amount of individual teaching which went on in relation to the "subjects" but these ten teachers appeared to confine this to the free choice period alone.

Of the other twenty teachers, fourteen are reported as making many links and as considering this matter to be of great importance — of these, five of the teachers work with a free or very flexible time-table.

The remaining six teachers make some links, but tend to confine this to one subject, chiefly "creative writing" where the children tend to write about what they have done in the free choice time.

One is reported as making links with both reading and number and another with discussion periods only.

The carry-over into the free choice period of interests developed during other times is reported chiefly in relation to stories which have stimulated dramatic play or model making. In one case scripture stories produced much activity.

With the fourteen teachers who make frequent links there is frequent mention of:

Creative writing and "News" books and letter writing
Reading — (the provision of books, and news sheets in relation to children's interests)
Number (weighing, measuring and calculating costs of material)
Stories chosen and talks given in relation to interests revealed in free choice periods.

There is also frequent mention of "all subjects" and many instances are given of links with geography, science, nature study, drama, art and craft. On the whole, however, though when special times of day are given to such work it is reported here, the evidence of the kind of help offered by the teacher has already been reported in the preceding chapter and need not be given again.

Observations were made as to whether the links between the free choice period and other activities were initiated by the teacher or by a child or group of children and the reports show a fairly equal division between teacher and child initiation and other examples where there was an almost even balance between the two.

EXAMPLES

Teacher Initiated

The teacher wanted to teach the children about money so she suggested that they should have a "snack bar" in the classroom. This involved making of cakes and pastries which caused the need to learn to use weights and measures — also the making of cushions for the chairs involved measuring and use of rulers. The front of the shop was made in wood and the awning painted. The teacher used other time for making a price list on the blackboard which children practised reading. They also had to suggest appropriate prices and learn how to make bills, so bringing in work in writing and arithmetic.

Child Initiated

In news time a child talked about his post office, how it was made and what envelopes he had collected for sorting. He mentioned post marks. This topic interested other children and the teacher took it up. This led to the need to know the alphabet for sorting the envelopes and an interest in the places from which they had come. Some were from places known by the children who then described them, others required the use of a map. Further interests arose in relation to stamps and their prices and to foreign countries in this connection.

Child – Teacher

Teacher watched a child drawing a train — suggested that a model should be made which also interested other children. This involved use of wood and nails, the sewing of red and green flags, and dressing up material, making and selling tickets, dramatic play and the production of a "Railway book", wall charts and the painting of railway posters.

Teacher – Child (reciprocal)

The teacher having told the children about Easter Gardens, the children decided they wanted to make one and made models. The teacher led this into the planting of grass and bulbs and the teaching of Easter stories and a hymn thus making links with nature study, scripture and singing.

In all these examples it is clear that the teacher played a very important part. As one observer remarks, "Activities cannot be linked with other forms of learning unless encouraged or stimulated by the teacher. If the teacher makes no attempt to follow the interests of the children then their enthusiasm wanes. But if the teacher understands her children, knows their interests and can arouse their enthusiasm, then wonderful results can be seen."

B. Examination of the question of record keeping by the teacher

For this investigation it was necessary to interview Head teachers as well as class teachers since some Head teachers required certain records to be made by the staff or relieved the staff at some part of this work by compiling certain "official" records themselves. In some areas there was a general practice of collecting and passing on to the Junior School certain general information about the children, together with particulars of their attainments in the skills of reading, writing and arithmetic. Class teachers sometimes gave the information verbally to the Head teacher.

With regard to other forms of record keeping the position varied a good deal, but only two of the thirty teachers who were interviewed kept no records at all, one of these was teaching in a small rural school where the children were very well known personally and where the teacher kept the children's books which she said was a sufficient record of their attainments and she had no difficulty, being fully aware of their interests and personal characteristics and needs. The other was a sad story of a keen teacher who had begun by keeping several records which had incurred criticism from other members of staff, who felt challenged by this, and so she decided "for the sake of peace" to follow her colleagues' practice in not keeping them!

Of the other twenty-eight teachers, the following table gives a broad description of their practice.

1. Keeps many records including (a) a weekly report of the main developments in the free choice period together with a forecast of expected developments, (b) an individual record of each child's background, personality, special interests and attainments and (c) notes of each child's present achievements in the basic skills especially reading and number.

6 Teachers

2. Keeps records together with plan or "forecast" of free choice periods together with records of achievements in the basic skills.

5 Teachers

3. Keeps only individual records on each child which include background, personality, interests and attainments in reading, arithmetic, etc.

4 Teachers

4. Keeps only records of the "activity" (i.e. free choice) period together with plans and forecast of probable developments.

1 Teacher

5. Keeps a brief weekly record and forecast of activities and a detailed record of attainments in reading.

2 Teachers

6. Keeps a weekly forecast of activities and records in both reading and arithmetic.

2 Teachers

7. Keeps records of reading and arithmetic and also of each child's creative ability.

1 Teacher

8. Keeps records only of attainments in reading, arithmetic and sometimes written English except that one teacher also records attainments in physical education.

7 Teachers

If one includes, as it seems right to do, the four teachers in category 3 who record fully the interests of individual children, it appears that two-thirds of the teachers find it desirable to make records of what is revealed in the free choice periods. These four, however, do not make specific written forecasts of how the interests will be followed up.

Some of the Head teachers stressed the importance of such records and planning, which range from the rough "diary" kept ready to hand in the classroom in which the teacher jots down observations and developments as they occur or at the first convenient moment afterwards, to a regular review of what has happened during the past week. In both cases these records contain suggestions for a follow up of various activities and reminders of material and equipment needed to further a child's purposes. Head teachers too sometimes glance through these records and are able, as a result, to offer helpful suggestions. One Head teacher commented on the danger of teachers in their enthusiasm spending too much time on recording at great length, but another described such work as "Time well spent in trying to evaluate the experience the children are getting, if one wants to maintain a sense of direction and ensure progress in the very 'free' situation". She added that under normal conditions it should not take a teacher more than an hour a week to keep the kind of records she asked for in this connection, though the individual records passed in at the end of each term were more time absorbing. She said that the better teachers often undertook, for their own satisfaction, more than the minimum asked for. She said the accepting of a weekly record can, in different ways, help many teachers, "reassuring the nervous, encouraging the stronger and in some measure keeping the potentially casual nearer to the mark."

There was no doubt that the class teachers as well as the Head teachers who did keep this type of record found it valuable to do so. On the other hand it must also be noted that one-third of the teachers did not do so, though there were only three who did not keep records of children's achievements in reading and arithmetic.

One observer commented as follows:
"Some teachers said they were sure that they knew exactly what was going on and what progress individuals were making without any need for the formality of writing things down and in some classrooms it was evident that they were indeed pretty knowledgeable about what was going on generally and also that they knew quite a lot about individual children." This is undoubtedly true of the teachers selected for this study, but the observer began her work by making a more general survey in less selected classrooms and states "In other cases there was more evidence of casualness and a more haphazard approach" and it seemed there that record keeping would have been desirable. It is possible that whether a good teacher does or does not need to write records of the free choice periods depends on her type of memory and possibly also on her enthusiasm and experience. Some teachers said they often thought about their work while they were washing up or cooking and some said they often chatted about the children and their work in the staffroom. It is not possible to estimate however whether the work, even of these good teachers, might have been improved still further had they kept records.

C. How far do the teachers make use of discussion periods in relation to "free choice" periods?

The technique of using a discussion period following a period of free choice is very often considered to be of great value when children have passed the age of six, when their purposes are more likely to call for planning ahead and when they are more interested in the contributions of other children than is the case with five-year-olds. On the whole we found that teachers of five-year-olds found it best to discuss situations only informally, as they arose with individual or small groups of children, rather than to attempt to conduct discussion periods with the whole class. Except for four teachers whose classes did contain some five-year-olds, this question has been investigated with teachers of children over six. The teachers of the four youngest classes include two who, like the other teachers of five-year-olds, do not use a separate discussion period, but one who does and the fourth who has developed a device of occasionally calling the class together during a period of free choice to discuss a common problem or the problem of a particular child or group of children. Her class was a small one of only twenty-four children. The other twenty-nine teachers include fifteen who hold systematic discussion periods in relation to periods when the children have had free choice of activity immediately after the free choice time though one teacher holds it only twice a week and others would feel free to allow the actual activities to overlap into the time on occasions. However, the period is greatly valued by these teachers and is used for appreciation of what children have been doing, letting children show and discuss their work with the group as a whole and for thinking out future plans, rectifying mistakes and enlisting the co-operation of other children in seeking information or material and helping to solve problems. One observer comments that the teacher uses this period to "let the children think, talk and extend their ideas" and another refers especially to the teacher's use of the period for "encouragement, praise and the pooling of ideas".

Two other teachers are reported as having no definite period for discussion of free activities, but as sometimes using a period described as "News" for that purpose, as well as for more general items of children's home interests or outside events.

The remaining twelve teachers depend solely on informal discussion with individuals or small groups of children during the free choice period itself and when one considers the high value ascribed to the discussion period by many teachers of six- and seven-year-old children, one wonders whether the ten teachers of classes of these ages are deprived of a valuable opportunity in having no such time available. These teachers (as do all the others) usually have "Language" or "News" periods on their time tables, but in some cases not immediately following the free choice time and it appears that they are used entirely for other purposes such as general news or work in English language. However, it should be noted that of these twelve teachers, only four are teaching children over seven and it is possible that some of those teaching six-year-olds believe that they, too, like the five-year-olds, are best served by informal discussion while activities are in progress and would not make such profitable use of a discussion period or that classes of less gifted six-year-olds are less able to do so than more gifted children of this age. The age groups are spread as follows:

	Systematic provision of period for discussing free activities	No period provided
Children aged 7–8	7	4
„ „ 6–7	7	6
„ „ 5–6	1	2

Discussion combined with News Period

One class aged 7+ and one 6+ gathered together occasionally during free choice period.
one class aged 5–6 also

CONCLUDING NOTE

The enquiries described above relate to the techniques of good informal teaching. It must not be thought that because it has been considered to be both useful and possible to look into these, that we are unaware of the much more deep and fundamental essentials of the work of any good teacher. The question of personal relationships with the children as individuals and as a group and with the children's parents are vital matters, but not susceptible to this type of investigation. The attributes of the teachers themselves, though briefly described in the following chapter, give only a slight indication of such qualities as a delight in children, a deep sense of purpose, an interest in life and a wealth of values which enrich and explain the teachers' actions and choices. Good techniques alone will not make a good teacher, but good teachers tend to value good techniques and to appreciate studying these in the work of other good teachers and to discover them afresh in their own work when they see them illustrated by other teachers under different conditions. One teacher, on reading the records we have gathered, made the remark "Yes, I can see I do nearly all these things but I did not realise it and it makes my work seem so much more worth while."

CHAPTER VII

Description of some of the teachers

A. INFANT SCHOOL STUDY

AN analysis was made from the descriptions contributed by the observers of thirty teachers to discover particularly frequent occurrence of any special characteristics of the teachers' background, personality traits, and the conditions under which they worked, as well as particular uses of certain techniques such as those already reported on (the use made of discussion periods, record keeping and links between the free choice period and the "subjects" of the curriculum).

Interviews were also held with the teachers in order to assess their own opinions on the advantages and difficulties inherent in this way of teaching and the matters on which they thought the teacher's emphasis should be laid.

To report first on the conditions under which the work of the teachers was carried out, the most outstanding common characteristics were that all, or nearly all, the teachers worked with the two great advantages of a good keen and sympathetic Head teacher and of a generous and varied supply of material and equipment. In only one case was the description of equipment given as less than "good" and that was described as "fair". Very often the phrase "very good" was used, sometimes with detailed lists of what was available and sometimes the phrase "equipment good and varied in spite of limited space" is given.

Descriptions of the Head teachers are equally favourable though in some cases the Head had only been in the school a short time and was too preoccupied with problems of organisation and initiating new members of staff and admitting new children to have much time for other matters, and the good work carried on by the teachers seemed to be done largely on their own initiative. In most cases, however, the Head teacher is mentioned as giving inspiration and sympathetic help. In no case was there any reference to a Head teacher being opposed to informal methods, though in two cases the period allowed for free choice was strictly limited to one hour each day.

In seventeen cases the normal daily time allowed for free choice was the first hour in the morning. In two other cases the hour varied between being given in the morning and afternoon sessions. In eleven schools the daily period was longer, the time assigned to it ranging from $1\frac{1}{2}$ to $2\frac{1}{2}$ hours. In the remaining two schools the five-year-olds had a second free choice period in the afternoons while the older children had only the first hour in the mornings. In five cases observers made special mention of the time-table being "flexible" or "informal".

With regard to buildings, there was a greater variation in the conditions under which the teachers succeeded in doing good work. Some buildings are described as "old and overcrowded", "old and classrooms small, but well arranged", others are described as "old and ugly, but classroom space good", or "old but well adapted". Other "new" buildings though attractive have smaller classrooms than some of the older buildings and others are both new and spacious. While only four of the teachers are described as having very poor classroom space in old buildings, considerably more than four have less space than is really desirable if large classes are to move about freely and have enough space for their creative work. Only twelve of the teachers have classes of less than forty children and, except for one teacher of maladjusted and backward children who has twenty-seven, only three have classes of less than thirty-six children. Eleven teachers have classes of over forty children, one having as many as fifty-two.

Outdoor space again varies and is on the whole less satisfactory than classroom space. In eight cases the description is "limited and no easy access to it". In other cases it is described as "good, but no access" or "playground only", but in other cases delightful gardens, spacious playgrounds and easy access are described. There are, however, only ten of the wholly favourable descriptions, and six observers have made no comment on outdoor space.

It is, I think, clear that in regard neither to adequate space nor to numbers in their classes could one say that the majority of the teachers were working under "ideal conditions". In eight cases a general comment was made to the effect that the teachers were working under difficult conditions. Only one is mentioned as outstandingly good.

With regard to the social background of the children, this too differs considerably. Four teachers have children described as coming from good working class or professional workers' families, eight are teaching children of very varied social background and six have children from a poor social neighbourhood. Seven others have a variation which includes a number of foreign children and the others are receiving children from new housing estates which contain families often unaccustomed to living together as neighbours.

A similar variation is found in the type of training undertaken by the teachers. Eight took the "Emergency" shortened training (of about 15 months) after the war, one of whom had subsequently gone on to take the Higher Froebel certificate. One teacher had taken a one-year training after serving as an uncertificated teacher and another a one-year training after obtaining a University Degree. Two teachers had taken a three-year Froebel training and the others a two-year training, though of these three had added another period of study, one to take an advanced course in Child Development, one an Art Teachers' Diploma and another the Higher Froebel certificate.

The teachers appeared to have a wide variety of out-of-school interests. Many of these entailed study; music was taken by five teachers, dancing classes by five others and "movement" by one. Seven others were taking courses in art or crafts of various kinds, two in psychology and education, and one in cookery. Out-of-school hobbies were also varied — gardening, keeping dogs, rock climbing, games and sports, and yachting, were mentioned as were also theatre and travel. Three teachers were doing social work with children (two with spastic children) and one mentioned Church work.

The personal attributes of the teachers, as reported on spontaneously by the observers, were analysed and are given below in order of the frequency with which they occurred.

There is obviously a great deal of overlap due to the slightly different wording in which observers reported what seemed to be the most outstanding characteristics of the teachers they observed and it is evident, for example, that had I put together all those which indicate a keen interest in children it would be clear that this was true of every teacher. There seems, however, some value in illustrating the variety of ways in which this tendency impressed the observers when describing different teachers. Owing to the frequency with which this interest in the children was reported I have listed together all descriptions which seem to have a bearing on this particular characteristic of the teachers. They are as follows:

	No. of times mentioned
1. Shows great regard for the children as individuals.	6
2. Understands and loves children.	5
3. Knows the childrens' needs very well.	5
4. Enjoys the childrens' company (one observer states "treats the children as valued friends").	4

L

	No. of times mentioned
5. Very ready to help children in difficulties.	4
6. Shows great patience.	4
7. Inspires trust.	3
8. Encourages the children to think for themselves.	3
9. Often shows affection.	3
10. Tries to understand the child's emotional needs.	3
11. Shows a sensitive awareness of the children's needs.	2
12. Is a sympathetic listener.	2
13. Shows sympathy.	2
14. Is among the children all the time.	2
15. Is motherly.	2
16. Is friendly.	1
17. Often comforts.	1
18. Often praises.	1
19. Sees the need to help the bright child as well as the dull.	1
20. Encourages very good co-operation between children.	1

Some qualities of the teachers were described at greater length and are not easy to list in summarised form but are too important to omit. One quality which comes out very strongly in many accounts of the teachers is the amount of thought they were devoting to their work — again and again one finds the pictures of their intervention being purposeful and based both on the appreciation of educational values and upon a very good knowledge of the children. Another quality which emerges is that the teachers are very resourceful and quick to exploit for the children's advantage the situations which arise. Though the qualities of serenity and patience are often mentioned they are actively rather than passively shown. For example, teachers will not merely endure with patience outside interruptions or mistakes made by children, but make use of them as a growing point of learning or thinking for the children.

Descriptions of the teachers often refer also to their personal attractiveness and their friendliness with colleagues and sympathetic attitude to children's parents, though opportunities for actual observation of the Infant School teachers with the children's parents are fewer than in the Nursery.

Other traits described which seem possible to list are as follows:

	No. of times mentioned
1. Outstanding evidence of interest in the children (already mentioned as the most frequently recorded trait).	24
2. Friendly, easy manner and charm.	13
3. Lively and alert.	13
4. Calm and serene.	12
5. Good organiser.	9
6. Quiet manner.	9
7. Cheerful and happy.	8
8. Firm discipline.	7
9. Warm and sympathetic.	6
10. Sense of humour.	5
11. Soft and pleasant voice.	4
12. Energetic.	4
13. Outstanding intelligence.	3
14. Eloquent.	2
15. Experimental.	2
16. Creative.	2
17. Self-controlled.	2
18. Reserved.	1
19. Reassuring.	1
20. Not demonstrative.	1

It should be emphasised that no directives were given to the observers who were left to give their own descriptions of what appeared to them most characteristic. Had they been supplied with the above list and asked to indicate the presence of any of the qualities it is most probable that certain categories would have come higher. Allowance must of course be made for the differences in the perceptiveness of observers. Many more than four of the teachers, for example, probably had pleasant voices, but observers did not always think of remarking on the voice. Where, however, characteristics are noted by many observers there is less reason to doubt that they were strongly evident than to have reservations about numbers in the lower categories.

Descriptions of a few of the teachers are given in full by way of illustration of the type of record from which the above conclusions have been compiled.

Short descriptions of two young teachers

1. *Description of Teacher A. and Description of Her Classroom. Age of children 6 years.*

Miss A. has been teaching at this school for about a year. She was sent as a temporary teacher, but the Headmistress was so delighted with her work that she asked for her to be a permanent member of staff. Miss A. is 26 and had a two-year training in 1952–4, at a College where the Principal herself was a pioneer in the education of young children. This teacher has obviously been inspired by the aims and principles that were given to her during her training. She has a delightful relationship with the children, at all times patient and understanding and always aware of the importance of education, in its widest sense. She has a very pleasant voice and quiet manner.

Miss A. is a very creative person and her room is always attractive and provides a very instructive environment that offers great scope for the children's intellectual development. She takes every opportunity that is presented to encourage the children to think for themselves, and to stimulate them to further enquiry. For example, she had put up this notice: "If you make something that is interesting put it on this table and then write about how you made it." The response from Derek was: "I made a telescope. First I got a tube and I got two cotton reels. Then I put them in the tube to make the eye piece. I made a stand by fixing two boxes together. Then I decided to paint the funnel. Then I painted the stand. One red knob is for adjusting the site and the others are for moving the site round."

Miss A. is very keen on outdoor activities. She is a good tennis player, enjoys rock climbing and yachting. The children's vocabulary and knowledge is often enlarged by the descriptions of her activities. She is also very fond of animals and this is evident in the classroom. She has this term taken her kitten to school each day and she prepared the children for this interest by putting this notice in the room: "Miss A. has had a little ginger kitten for an Easter present, and she is going to bring it to school in a basket after Easter. Find out how to look after and feed kittens and write about it here."

Her room is always prepared before the children arrive in the morning. The activities available are painting, clay, cooking, shopping, woodwork, bricks, crayoning, construction with junk material, sewing, home corner, and book corner. From time to time there are additional activities that have been initiated by the children, for example the interest in puppets, a Post Office, an Easter garden, and a train.

The children work in the classroom, the corridor and in the court-yard adjoining the classroom. They are usually given about a quarter of an hour in which to pack up and following that, there is a discussion period in which the children describe the work that they have been doing and if necessary ask for help on any particular problem that they have. If any child is particularly absorbed in his task, he is quite free to continue after the Assembly and break time.

This Head teacher now runs Saturday morning courses on Activity Methods for teachers under the particular Education Authority for whom she is working. These are very well attended.

2. *Miss X.*

Miss X. is an Emergency trained Teacher, and about 28 years' old. She gave up a good post to train to be a teacher. She has been trained in Activity Methods and is unfamiliar with the old régime. She travels an hour every morning so as to teach in an Activity School, as she feels herself she would not be successful in a formal atmosphere.

One may feel that this young teacher with only four years' experience may not come under the category of a good teacher. On the contrary, I felt that she is an extremely capable teacher, who knows where she is going, shows foresight, initiative and wise judgments. Her manner with the children is extremely good. She is not forceful, you hardly hear her, but she is always at hand, suggesting, stimulating, helping, encouraging, advising and demonstrating. She never raises her voice, but has only to say, in her subdued tone, "Children, I want to talk to you," and a hush falls over the entire room. They respect her, and know she has something worthwhile to tell them.

The apparatus in this room is good, bright and attractive and appeals to the children. She provides unlimited material for the junk box, and spends much of her time in preparing material and apparatus for her class. Whenever I have stayed during play-time and dinner hour, I have always found her happily preparing for the next period of work. She clearly has the children's interests at heart.

I was particularly interested to discover Miss X. attends Pottery classes once a week purely for pleasure. I was amazed at the interest in clay pots, vases and bowls in the class, which was reflected from the teacher. This reveals itself in the periods I sampled. One day she mentioned to the class that she wanted to catch a train, and they were eager to know where she was going. She told them about her pottery class, and the next day they wanted to know all about her evening's work, and straight away set to to make clay pots of their own. This

L*

interest has grown and practically every child has made a clay pot, painted and varnished them; and every home boasts of a hand-made pot. These pots are particularly gay and attractive.

A longer description of an older teacher

Teacher B. (Teaching children aged 6½–7½ years)

Teacher B. came to this school when she left college 16 years previously when the school was newly opened. Throughout this time she had been experimenting along various lines of activity, and during the past two years the only fixed times have been for assembly and religious instruction and one period in the hall each day for music.

This teacher was always very natural with her children and had unbounded energy. From the beginning of the morning until the last thing in the afternoon she was constantly "feeding into" to children's activities and individual interests, thus enabling each child to develop his interests from day to day, with the result that not only was this class of 45 children working very steadily but the children's work reached a very high standard. The interests of the children and their range of knowledge was amazingly wide, ranging from interest in the variety of materials offered, to such topics as stamp collecting, guide books of Lancashire, Yorkshire and the British Isles, and the route to India. It may be of interest to note here that not only was this teacher feeding individual interests with great energy throughout the day but much of her spare time was necessarily spent in finding and making suggestive books and collections of materials and perhaps her great success with these children was mainly due to her deep interest in every phase of the development of each of her children's interests. Minute recording of individual interests had been found by the staff of this school to be quite unnecessary owing to the fact that with these conditions of free work throughout the day, the teachers come to know each of their children well. Teacher B. kept detailed records of the difficult children in her class and of those with special problems. A general survey of the main interest in her class was written from time to time. In this way, time spent on recording was kept to the minimum, and, as I have said, in the case of this particular teacher, most of her own time was spent not in recording but in the preparation and collection of stimuli and information which enabled individuals to maintain their interest.

She was intensely interested in the children's development in music. Though she could play the piano well, and did so for recorder practices, percussion instruments and in particular an Indian tom-

tom were used for movement which was again at a very high standard. The children thoroughly enjoyed this work moving as they did with great freedom of movement and expressing their ideas most unselfconsciously.

Class discussions were arranged as they were needed, sometimes once or perhaps twice a week. During my visits only one discussion was arranged, which lasted about 30 minutes. On another occasion impromptu discussion arose which took about 5 minutes. There were no other discussions.

The work of Teacher B., from all accounts, was not influenced in any way by the presence of the observer. The observer was invited to come and go as frequently as she wished so that often when the teacher was busy, most of a time-sample would be taken before the teacher realised that the observer was in the room. On more than one occasion she volunteered the information that during her years of teaching she had never had a visitor whose presence disturbed her and her class less than that of the observer.

Teacher B. had a natural and easy relationship with every child in her class. There were in this class, two boys who were outstandingly difficult though for very different reasons. On the part of one boy the difficulty may be traced to his home background. On days when one or other and sometimes both of these boys were very unsettled and showing signs of disturbance Teacher B. often asked if she should suggest work for them and on these occasions, when they were given a set task, it certainly did seem to help them to become more calm and settled. Teacher B. kindly and firmly insisted and helped them to complete such a task once they had started. Her records, which the observer was invited to read, contained details of the children's difficulties and progress and were written with sympathy and deep understanding.

This teacher had in her classroom an amazingly large collection of materials and reference books. Whatever a child needed seemed always to be at hand. All of these materials were easily available on shelves or tables round the room. Generally, the children went to the shelves to take whatever they needed. As they came in at the beginning of the morning the children tended to gather in groups and have a friendly chat before the register was called. It was a rule in this class that all the children stopped whatever they were doing quickly when it was time for registration and this was followed quickly by collecting dinner money. The children were always very quiet and Teacher B. felt that much less time was lost by stopping everyone and doing this quickly all together, than by trying at the same time to cope both with children and administration.

It has also been found by this teacher that classes of children varied in the way they began the day. The present group always seemed to like to chat to each other first on arrival, while the group which this same teacher had had last year came into the room and at once began to work along various lines of activity.

This teacher was not afraid to offer suggestions and on occasions to demonstrate a skill when this was necessary. Although her behaviour with the children was always easy and natural, she could be very firm when necessary. The children responded easily to her and were obviously devoted to her.

A vast amount of general knowledge and factual information on a variety of subjects arose during the discussions which were most skilfully led. Ideas were stimulated, and shared, experiences collected and widened.

Her real affection for the children showed itself in her untiring efforts on their behalf to stimulate and to encourage, her sensitivity and quickness to sense their need for help over a difficult patch, and her very real sympathy, expressed both by words of comfort and a caress, when a child was hurt or unhappy.

There was a very friendly and happy atmosphere in the classroom. The teacher had a very happy disposition and was always ready to laugh with the children. For instance, on one occasion, when Miss B. had been explaining to a child where she had gone wrong, the child suddenly burst out laughing and said "Oh, heck", whereupon Miss B. laughed heartily, remarking to the child and smiling at the observer, "Oh, don't let Miss O. hear you say 'Oh, heck', she will think we are a lot of barbarians."

There were no set times for physical education, the children were free to use the climbing apparatus and small apparatus whenever they wished. In order to supervise the outdoor work, a helper was attached to this top class. Woodwork also took place outside. As well as this general outdoor supervision, the helper also helped Teacher B. to make, replace, or mend classroom equipment and to do any other odd jobs that were needed. This teacher said that it was undoubtedly a great advantage to have someone attached to her class for such purposes and that it helped her enormously to feel that she could give practically her whole attention to the work of the children in the classroom, knowing that those who went into the playground from time to time were adequately supervised. Some children also went into the hall from time to time or into the music room to practise music and dancing. Many composed their own melodies and wrote these down. Many dances were made up, also.

This teacher had a very large and varied supply of reference materials which were almost constantly in use by the children. All the apparatus and collections, including the nature table, were well cared for and tidily kept. It is essential that in a room such as this, where there was an abundance of material which must be quickly available and which was constantly in use, that there must be good organisation of every inch of available space and, of course, it must be tidy.

Miss B. respected her children and they certainly respected her. She welcomed the children when they came into the room in the morning and often said "Please" or "Thank you" or asked a child's permission before looking at a piece of work and on one occasion, for example, when a child was writing a letter to her and Miss B passed by before it was finished, she smiled at the child who put her hand over it, protesting and reassuring her, "But I wouldn't dream of reading it, darling, if you don't want me to." This letter was "posted" to her later as a surprise. She never forgot earnestly to thank a child when a letter was written to her and frequently wrote letters or sent, through the class post office, parcels containing new ideas or sometime to stimulate an interest. These letters and parcels were written and made up in her spare time, usually at home, as was most of her preparation.

Although this teacher admits that forecasting of such work is not possible, at the same time she keeps ahead of each child's needs by collecting together whatever she thinks might be needed if the interest develops in the way she thinks it might, though she never imposes her ideas upon the children. It is simply a case of looking ahead in order to be able to provide for these needs when the occasion arises.

This teacher proved to be by far the most tiring of the three on which to take records for she spoke quickly and moved from one child to another very quickly. Sometimes her attention was divided among about three children at once.

B. NURSERY SCHOOL STUDY

Miss Cass examined the records of the observers in the Nursery Schools and gives the following report, together with some general comments.

Qualities as observed in the teachers in the Nursery School Study

Although eighteen teachers are not a large number from which to draw conclusions it is interesting to see the differences between them and how the varying categories of contacts were used by them.

Teacher C. with the highest score of contacts of all the eighteen teachers does appear to be the most mature and successful of all the individuals observed, and so perhaps it is pertinent to use her as an example to illustrate many of the qualities which were found.

A high score of contacts is not, however, necesarily a criterion of excellence. Children can be overwhelmed with smothering love, fed with unsuitable and indigestible intellectual information, never left to play independently, and have demands made on them for acceptable behaviour, good manners, attention to routines, etc., which are in no way suitable to their age and development. However, it is not only the high number of contacts made by Teacher C. that strike one, it is their quality and kind, and the general picture of her playroom and personality which emerges. She had a group of 30 children with an average attendance of 25 and she had no two-year-olds in the group when these observations were made.

Teacher C. gave the impression of being a thoroughly happy person, young (about 26) active and lively but not fussy. Her mood was stable and her attitude consistent to both children and adults, and she was always very welcoming. She was smiling and cheerful and yet had an inner quietness which allowed the children, as it were, to blossom. She obviously felt that the development of good social attitudes and social awareness were important, and she made the highest score in this category of all the eighteen teachers. She also scored highly in categories showing a warm and loving response and acceptance of the child, and a building up of his feelings of adequacy and confidence. There was a notable lack of "fuss" in this group and when C. gave her attention to a child or to a group of children she gave it very fully and appeared at leisure to carry on a really long and satisfactorily completed conversation. Instances of disputes were rare in this group and tended to be settled in a positive way.

EXAMPLE

Sarah and new Janet both wanted to play with the same thing in the Wendy House —
  Janet: "Miss C., she won't let me."
  C.: "Look, Sarah, this is Janet, and she wants to play, too."
  Sarah: "I'm the mummy."
  C.: "Sometimes there are two mummies in one house, one up and one downstairs, or, Janet, perhaps you can be Auntie."

Any kind of rejection or refusal by C. was rare, and she had a way of "softening the blow" or saving the child's face which went far to helping him.

EXAMPLE

Andrew was spoiling the group's singing, and C. asked him not to, but she added, "Sing nicely, like you usually do."

If a child had to wait a turn, C. suggested an alternative, or gave hope to a child that he would soon have his desire.

EXAMPLE

Maurice wanted to make a fifth at the clay table.

C.: "No we can only have four, Maurice, or else the clay goes on the floor, Would you like to look at books just here, and then when one of these has finished you'll be able to come, perhaps someone won't be very long."

So often C.'s explanations put the social point of view, drawing attention to other people's feelings, and showing consideration for their convenience or happiness. She also showed a genuine sharing of her feelings and ideas with those of the children and she not only sympathised with them, joining in with their joy or sorrow, she also shared such of her own feelings as were capable of being understood by the children concerned. The children across the room in the rocking boat were singing, "Golden Slumbers", C. joined in and sang across to them. She also had an intuitive sensing of the needs of the group. Rita, a four-year-old, had had a small fire in her house the evening before. Throughout the period she was constantly approaching C. with information about the fire and C. was very generous in giving Rita the attention she needed. She listened to lengthy accounts, introduced opportunities for Rita to tell others of her experiences, suggested that Rita paint a picture of her fire and then wrote down the story of the picture at Rita's dictation. C. also scored highly in the giving of intellectual information to the children, though she did not overwhelm them with unwanted material, and her score in N.1 is not as high as Teacher D. On the other hand she scores highly in ,"inviting spontaneous information and ideas" from the child himself.

If teacher C., with the highest score of contacts, was perhaps the most mature and well-balanced of all those teachers observed, interesting differences of technique and personality which was often enriching to the children, appeared in the observations of the other seventeen teachers.

One got the impression from one or two of the teachers that they envisaged the Nursery School rather as a children's workshop, and much of their time was spent in supplying information, encouraging skills, or suggesting additions to the children's productions.

New words would be introduced to them. Bobby, aged four, said something about a window and the teacher told him that "windows in boats are called portholes". Their attention would be drawn to new and interesting things around them; a musical box was put on the table when a group of children were drinking their milk and the teacher asked them to "listen to the music". Sometimes one felt that children were a little overwhelmed when words and suggestions were made that were unacceptable. One teacher, anxious perhaps to lead a child on to more creative efforts, said brightly as she looked at what he was doing with his clay, "That's a lovely handle on your cup. Are you going to make a saucer?" "No", said the child firmly, "it's a mug". Play too can be over-directed and lose its spontaneity, and a teacher can artificially stimulate an activity which the children have really out-lived. Good teachers learn to avoid these pitfalls, but in process of developing the art of giving the right and not the wrong kind of stimulus some mistakes are made at first. Sometimes one felt that a teacher was uncertain of her own rôle and function, not knowing when to step in and when to stand back and sometimes this meant that she concerned herself with the equipment and materials rather than with the children, feeling perhaps that this was safer. This sometimes resulted in over concern in the general order and tidiness of the room. Children will certainly need to be reminded to put things away, wipe up spills, keep sand off the floor, wash their hands, etc., but to be constantly demanding a rather adult-orientated conception of neat and tidy play can be exhausting and unproductive for everybody.

A teacher too can sometimes hurry a child on to an activity of some kind before he is ready because he appears to be doing nothing. In point of fact the need to "stand and stare", to take something in, in order to make it one's own, to escape for a moment into an inner fantasy world, away from everyone and everything, is a very necessary part of growth.

Some groups of children seem to need more actual physical attention than others, and one teacher on a new housing estate appeared at first sight to be over-fussy about her children's physical needs and minor hurts. They were, however, an unsettled and rather insecure group and one gradually became aware that this particular teacher was giving, obviously with satisfaction, something of real value to these children. With some teachers it might have taken a slightly different form. This teacher, however, felt that this was the best contribution she could make to help them to develop feelings of security.

The skill required to anticipate children's needs is an important one, and some teachers possess this quality in very good measure. The child who isn't getting the help and notice he feels is his right can sometimes draw attention to himself in an awkward and time-consuming way.

Thus, one teacher often tended to arrive too late to prevent disaster, when a child had already spilt the paint or got himself wet through, as if he had almost unconsciously forced her to come to his aid and notice him. These sorts of incidents, if they continue to happen throughout the day, can be extremely wearing, and by the end of an afternoon both children and teacher can be over-tired and over-wrought, coping with accidents that could have been avoided.

One or two teachers seemed to feel that children should be left very much alone, to develop in their own way, rarely giving guidance, making suggestions or offering help.

No child, of course, wants his play to be dominated by the adult, nor does he want to be constantly told what to do. To find himself directed into one sort of play for one period and a different sort of play at another is very frustrating indeed. We are well aware today that children need long spells of uninterrupted play of their own choosing. On the other hand children cannot learn everything from each other, or by trying things out for themselves, and adult experience and knowledge should be available to them.

Obviously the teacher must provide a rich, exciting, secure and challenging environment suitable to the children's needs and also be ready with help, ideas, and information, where it is needed.

No teacher consciously denied children help when they requested it; sometimes they had to wait, but this is inevitable with a group of children. At times one felt, however, with one or two teachers that they stood back taking too passive a rôle, leaving their children to manage as best they could when either active interest, participation, a sharing of knowledge or a new approach suggested would have been welcomed by the children. One teacher who had a small group of rather young children — two- and three-year-olds with no four- and five-year-olds — did appear to find that she got very little stimulation back from her group. She actually said that she felt she was nothing but a glorified nurse-maid, and she gave the impression of being somewhat bored.

One can sympathise with her feelings, even if one does not agree with her general assumptions. It does emphasise the fact, however, that mixed age groups are, generally speaking, more satisfactory. They are more natural, better for the children and certainly more provocative and inspiring for the teacher.

The fact that the teacher's personal maturity is so important a factor in her ability to satisfy her children's demands really needs no research to prove, on the other hand it is of value perhaps to be able to underline it.

It is surprising how often the young, uncertain, immature and insecure teacher, sometimes straight from College, is given the youngest group of children in the school. In the Infants School it will be the reception class, in the Nursery School, if the children are in age groupings, it will be the two-year-olds. How often too do we still find the young Nursery Helper or the untrained Nursery Assistant in Nursery Schools, Day Nurseries and Residential Nurseries being given far too much responsibility and having to take major decisions. when they have neither the maturity, knowledge nor experience to do so.

We pay lip-service to the fact that the years under five are the most formative and vital period in a child's whole life and yet we often put them in the sole charge of adults or adolescents who know little about the deeper needs and problems of childhood and are still in the process of trying to cope with their own difficulties.

It must be remembered that young children's emotions are very near the surface and they show their feelings of aggression, hostility, jealousy, love and hate, often very spontaneously and freely in their behaviour to those around them. This can arouse all sorts of anxieties in the immature adult, bringing to the surface and reminding them, as it were, of many of their own unresolved conflicts and anxieties.

It is not enough, of course, just to say that a teacher must be mature, though this point has been emphasised. Certain specific qualities will obviously be more important and necessary than others in providing for the rather special needs of very young children, and these particular qualities do emerge in the personalities of the teachers selected and observed.

It was very obvious, for example, how necessary it was to be able to give and receive affection, to share and co-operate in the children's interests, pleasures, joys and sorrows, and there are countless examples of this ability with all the teachers observed. It was generally the less able individual who gave the most orders. One teacher was very anxious that her children should be independent, a very commendable thing. She did, however, give her children too many specific orders, "Mary go and wipe your face and hands", "John, put the bricks away", etc.

A more positive approach was used by the more secure teachers, who sought to gain their children's co-operation. If they wanted help, or a simple routine carried out, they would encourage independence rather than demand it.

All the teachers were aware of the need to encourage children in contacts likely to promote good social attitudes and an increase in social awareness. They realised that children could not be hurried in their social development, but that they could be helped by example and guidance and by the general feeling of ease, acceptance and working together in the Nursery. It was not always a good idea, however, to give children the impression, which sometimes occurred, that one only did something kind and thoughtful to somebody else because it might mean that they in return would do something kind and thoughtful back. Thus to say to a child, "Come here and hold this coat for Peter and help him, and then he will hold your coat for you", was a somewhat negative social approach, though probably better than nothing.

A number of the teachers showed special interest and admiration for the children's homes; clothes their mothers had made; things their fathers did; or their brothers and sisters had done. This made a real link for the children between school and home, teachers greeted parents warmly making them feel they were part of the Nursery School, and this was of real benefit to the children.

The playrooms and materials also reflected the personalities of the teachers. The teachers' own special interests were also apparent. One teacher who was very keen on children's paintings had a delightful and vivid collection in the room, while another had a room alive with plants and growing things.

Perhaps a short quotation from Dr. W. D. Wall's book, *Child of Our Time*, would make a suitable conclusion to this chapter. He says here, "The function of the good Nursery School, indeed is much more than the giving of suitable outlets and possibilities. We know enough of the way in which the mind and personality develop in the early years to surmise that the ways in which adults intervene, the kinds of experience they provide, and the general emotional stimulus which they give, have a profound influence upon intellectual and personal growth. This, of course, does not mean that there should be formal teaching. It does mean that the environment should be thought of as educational in its fullest sense. The work of the best Nursery School teacher, from Susan Isaacs onwards, has shown how, by interacting with children at the right moment, by stimulating them to games for which they are ready but which they would not find out for themselves, by conversation which skilfully enlarges their experience, by arrangement of the environment, and in many other ways, the development of children can be accelerated."

CHAPTER VIII

Opinions of the teachers

DURING the investigation it was possible to interview forty-nine Infant School teachers. Certain questions were asked of all the teachers, but they were allowed to talk freely and expand, or omit trying to search for answers if they felt there was nothing they had to contribute to a particular question. There was some inevitable over-lap in some of the replies and teachers naturally used slightly different wording, but the substance of the replies are given below:

The first question was:

"What is the function of the teacher in the active Infant School?"

	No. of times mentioned
To provide the right environment, materials and equipment.	16
To stimulate new interests and widen horizons.	11
To guide, help, encourage and advise.	7
To give child security.	7
To provide the opportunity for each child to develop fully (supply essentials for healthy growth).	6
To work through or use the child's interests.	5
To satisfy the needs of the child.	4
To create a happy atmosphere.	4
To organise materials well.	3
To provide the opportunity for each child to realise his potential.	3
To be aware of the child's needs.	3
To promote curiosity, exploration, desire to learn.	3
To encourage independence and good social behaviour.	3
To allow the child to develop at his own rate.	2
To allow the child to develop his creative ideas to the full.	2
To encourage a sense of responsibility, right attitudes.	2

	No. of times mentioned
To give affection.	1
To ensure each child has success in some field.	1
To help children to become individuals and thinking members of society.	1

One Head teacher summed it up —
"To provide the child with a 'live' day so he can be living, learning and growing all the time."

Another teacher said,
"To create an environment in which children may pursue with enjoyment their interests and occupations."

The second question was:

"What do children gain from active methods?"

The general opinion of all the teachers was best summed up by one Head teacher whose answer to me was — "Everything"! Another said, "They live life instead of watching it."

Expanding on these replies, the following points were mentioned:

	No. of times mentioned
Children have opportunity to develop at their own rate.	14
Children gain in confidence, independence and initiative.	13
Children have opportunity for all-round development.	8
Children learn to work together, to co-operate, to share.	7
Children can follow their own interests.	4
Children learn more easily by experience.	4
Children benefit through learning from each other.	3
Children can develop creative ideas.	3
Children have opportunity to live more richly, it is more interesting for them.	3
Children have opportunity "to play out" problems.	2
Children learn to converse better.	2
Children have freedom to experiment.	1
Children have easy access to the teacher.	1

	No. of times mentioned
Children are treated as individuals.	1
Children can be more lively, contribute more	1
Children learn self-discipline.	1
Children feel loved.	1

The replies to the third question:

"Are there any advantages to the teacher in active methods?"

reflect the enthusiasm of the teachers to accomplish their task as successfully as possible. Most of their replies, which are concerned with advantages to the children, show how the teacher is helped in her task by using activity methods.

	No. of times mentioned
Teacher has time to know and understand individual children and their needs (more insight into character).	18
More interesting, lively and enjoyable for the teacher.	15
Teacher's relationship with child is easier, closer, friendlier (natural, pleasant atmosphere).	9
Teacher can help individual children with difficulties and problems.	8
Teacher can work at child's own rate, give individual attention.	6
More rewarding for the teacher, satisfaction of doing a job well.	5
Teacher can work from her own and the children's interests.	3
Teacher gets willing co-operation, enthusiasm and interest from children.	3
There is purpose in the whole scheme.	1

One teacher said:

"How different this is from the old days when everything was so rigid and formal! There's nothing to compare — it's so lovely, the feeling between you and the children. What a friendly relationship grows up between you, and how much better you get to know the children and their problems."

The fourth question was —

"Are there any disadvantages to the teacher in active methods?"

Twenty of the teachers considered that there were no disadvantages. The replies of the others were as follows:

	No. of times mentioned
Harder mentally and physically, more exhausting. Demands more hard work, time and energy.	20
Difficult to satisfy all the children's needs with a large class.	5
Needs more organisation.	5
Difficult to keep records.	2
Some difficulty and anxiety in giving practice in the basic skills.	2
Apprehensive children tend to be bewildered and need help to settle.	1

The fifth question was —

"Are there any improvements which you feel would make the active method more successful?"

This gave the teachers a chance to mention the size of classes which is a drawback in all Infant Schools.

	No. of times mentioned
Smaller classes.	22
Larger classrooms with better facilities.	9
More apparatus and materials, right equipment.	8
Fuller and deeper understanding of the "active" method.	7
Opportunity and time for refresher courses, study and visits.	4
Modern buildings.	3
More storage facilities.	2
Help with non-teaching duties.	2
Easy access from room to open air.	2

	No. of times mentioned
Playgrounds more interesting.	1
Confidence of parents in the method.	1
More careful selection of Infant School teachers.	1
Stock cupboard freely available at all times.	1
Greater understanding of teachers in the Junior School so more follow-up.	1

Only sixteen of the teachers were asked the next question which was:

"About how long do you spend per week, outside normal school hours, on school work, apparatus, etc.?"

Most of them said that it varied with the needs of the class and the interests and activities which developed during the week. Observers commented on the conscientiousness of the teachers and noted that rooms showed evidence of much preparation. Several of the teachers made a daily list of things to be done for the next day. Those who did state a definite time for preparation, etc., emphasised that it was only approximate.

	No. of teachers
2 hours per week	2
3 ,, ,, ,,	2
5 ,, ,, ,,	1
6 ,, ,, ,,	2
7 ,, ,, ,,	1
10 ,, ,, ,,	1

The final question:

"What improvements would you want to make in your classroom or school building if it were possible?"

was put to twenty-one teachers. Their replies depended, of course, upon the facilities they had, but, nevertheless, they show some of the requirements which help to make it easier for a teacher to use activity methods.

Sink with hot and cold water in classroom.	8
Easy access to open air (larger doors).	6
More storage space inside room (stock cupboard inside).	5

Larger room.	4
More display board on walls.	4
Large shed, or room, for storing big apparatus, spare furniture, gardening tools, animal food, clay, sand, etc.	4
Bungalow building, separate from Junior School.	3
Larger working surface (desks, tables).	2
Covered shelter in playground.	2
Stacking furniture.	1
Heated rail to dry wet clothes.	1

However, it is important to remember that all the teachers who expressed the views above were using "active" methods successfully without these amenities. Several worked in modern buildings but they had no large cupboard in the classroom and only a small door to the open air, through which it was difficult to carry equipment outside. Eight of the teachers, who worked in older buildings, had no sink in their classrooms but used buckets and bowls instead.

It is not ideal conditions which have enabled these teachers to work successfully, but their own enthusiasm, initiative and determination to overcome obstacles. But that is no reason why they should not be given encouragement, by the provision of good buildings and amenities, to enable them to fulfil their task with greater ease.

Bibliography

Selected books which deal with research in the subject

ANDERSON H. H., BREWER H. M. and REED M. F., *Studies of Teachers' Classroom Personalities* I, II and III, Applied Psychology Monographs VI, VIII and XI, California, Stanford University Press, 1945–46.

BIRKINSHAW M., *The Successful Teacher*, Hogarth Press, 1935.

CATTELL R. B., The Assessment of Teaching Ability, *British Journal of Educational Psychology*, February, 1931.

CAREY S. M., Evaluating Teaching Competence, *Elementary School Journal*, Vol. XLI, 1941.

EVANS K. M., A Critical Survey of Methods of Assessing Teaching Ability, *British Journal of Educational Psychology*, June, 1951.

FOSTER JOSEPHINE C., Distribution of the Teachers' Time Among Children in the Nursery School and Kindergarten, *Journal of Educational Research*, October, 1930.

GABRIEL JOHN, *An Analysis of the Emotional Problems of the Teacher in the Classroom*, Melbourne F. W., Cheshire, 1957.

HUGHES MARIE M., *Development of the Means for Assessing the Quality of Teaching in Elementary Schools*, U.S. Department of Health, Education and Welfare Office of Education, Washington 25, D C., 1959.

JENSEN A. C., Determining Critical Requirements for Teachers, *Journal of Experimental Education*, Vol. XX, September, 1951.

JERSILD A. T., GOLDMAN B., JERSILD C. L. and LOFTUS J. J., Studies of Elementary Classes in Action, *Journal of Experimental Education*, Vols. IX and X, June and December, 1941.

JONES MARGARET, Analysis of Certain Aspects of Teaching Ability, *Journal of Experimental Education*, Vol. XXV, December, 1956.

LEVIN H., HILTON T. and LEIDERMAN G., Studies of Teacher Behaviour, *Journal of Experimental Education*, Vol. XXVI, September, 1957.

LEWIN K., LIPPITT R. and WHITE R. K., Patterns of Aggressive Behaviour in Experimentally Created Social Climates, *Journal of Social Psychology*, Vol. X, May, 1939.

MONTROSS HAROLD W., Temperament and Teaching Success, *Journal of Experimental Education*, Vol. XXIII, September, 1954.

ROSTHER M. E., ROLFE J. F. and LADUKE C. V., The Measurement of Teaching Ability, *Journal of Experimental Education*, Vol. XIV, September, 1945.

RYANS DAVID G., The Criteria of Teaching Effectiveness, *Journal of Educational Research*, Vol. XLII, May, 1949.

A Study of the Extent of Association of Certain Professional and Personal Data with Judged Effectiveness of Teacher Behaviour, *Journal of Experimental Education*, Vol. XX, September, 1951.

SYMONDS PERCIVAL N., Personality of the Teacher, *Journal of Educational Research*, Vol. XL, May, 1947.

Reflections on Observations of Teachers, *Journal of Educational Research*, Vol. XLIII, May, 1950.

VON HADEN H. I., An Evaluation of Certain Types of Personal Data Employed in the Prediction of Teaching Efficiency, *Journal of Experimental Education*, Vol. XV, September, 1946.

Selected books on the education of young children which throw light on the rôle of the teacher

BOYCE E. R., *Play in the Infant School*, Methuen, 1938.
Infant School Activities, Nisbet, 1939.
The First Year in School, Nisbet, 1953.
CURTIS-DWIGHT K. and ANDREWS LEONARD O., *Guiding your Student Teacher*, New York, Prentice-Hall, 1954.
DENT H. C., *Changes in English Education*, University of London Press, 1952.
To be a Teacher, University of London Press, 1947.
DICKIE D., *The Enterprise in Theory and Practice*, Gage & Co., 1941.
EATON W. J., Social Science Approach to Nursery School Teaching and the Social Role of the Nursery School Teacher defined and explored, *Child Welfare*, 1955.
FOSTER and HEADLEY, *Education in the Kindergarten*, American Book Co., 1948.
GARDNER D. E. M., *Education of Young Children*, Methuen, 1956.
GLASSEY and WEEKES, *The Educational Development of Children*, University of London Press, 1958.
GRUNELIUS ELIZABETH M., *Educating the Young Child*, London, New Knowledge Books, 1956.
HICKS-HANNE J., *Administrative Leadership in the Elementary School*, New York, The Ronald Press Co., 1956.
HOCKETT and JACOBSEN, *Modern Practices in the Elementary School*, Ginn & Co., 1943.
HUME, *Learning and Teaching in the Infant School*, Longmans Green, 1938.
ISAACS SUSAN, *Intellectual Growth in Young Children*, Routledge, 1930.
JERSILD A., *When Teachers Face Themselves*, Teachers' College, Columbia University, 1955.
LANE, HOWARD and BEAUCHAMP MARY, *Human Relations in Teaching*, New York, Prentice-Hall, 1955.
LINDGREN H. C., *Educational Psychology in the Classroom*, London, Chapman & Hall; New York, J. Wiley, 1956.
MELLOR E., *Education Through Experience in the Infant School Years*, Blackwell, 1950.
MELVIN A. G., *The Activity Programme*, New York, Macmillan, 1946.
The Technique of Progressive Teaching, John Day, Reprinted, 1938.
MOUSTAKAS B. E., *The Teacher and the Child*, McGraw-Hill, 1956.
NATIONAL UNION OF TEACHERS, *Nursery and Infant Education*, Evans Bros., 1949.
Activity Methods for Children Under Eight, Evans Bros., 1950.
OHLSEN MERLE M., *Guidance — An Introduction*, New York, Harcourt, Brace & Co., 1955.
PORTER H. P., *The Teacher in the New School*, World Book Co., 1931.
RUSK ROBERT, N., *A History of Infant Education*, University of London Press, 1953.
SHEEY E. M., *The Fives and Sixes Go to School*, New York, Henry Holt & Co., 1955.
SIMPSON D. and ALDERSON D., *Creative Play in the Infant School*, Pitmans, 1950.
STEVENS B. P., *The Activities Curriculum in the Primary Grades*, New York, Heath Co., 1931.
THOMAS R. MURRAY, *Ways of Teaching in Elementary Schools*, New York, Longmans Green, 1955.
WOFFARD, *Teaching in Small Schools*, New York, Macmillan, 1946.